Mel Bay Presents

RIGHT-HAND ARPEGGIO STUDIES
for Acoustic Guitar

by Richard Matteson, Jr.

D1591560

1 2 3 4 5 6 7 8 9 0

Visit us on the Web at www.melbay.com — E-mail us at email@melbay.com

Table of Contents

Section One - Basic Forms and Technique

Basic Right Hand Movement

Simple Arpeggios
Sympathetic Movement Arpeggios; The Forward Rolls (p,i,m) (p,i,a) (p,m,a) (p,i,m,a)

Sympathetic Movement Arpeggios; The Backward Rolls (p,m,i) (p,a,i) (p,a,m) (p,a,m,i)

Sympathetic Movement Arpeggios; Tremolo

Complex Arpeggios

Section Two - The Arpeggio Reference Section

Arpeggio Bass Patterns

Section Three - Arpeggio Pieces

Foreword

Playing arpeggios is one of the most important right-hand techniques a fingerstyle or classical guitarist can develop. Rapid and secure arpeggios are essential ingredients in performing virtuoso fingerstyle and classical pieces.

This book, *Right-Hand Arpeggio Studies for Acoustic Guitar*, will present a thorough study of the essential arpeggio forms as well as technical information to develop the right-hand fingers.

This book doesn't teach you basic right-or left-hand technique or any fundamental details on how to play the guitar, it teaches you how to play arpeggios. If you are a beginner you should find a qualified teacher to help you with your right-hand position and basic finger movements.

All the exercises except for the sweep section are to be *played free stroke* with fingers and thumb. Most of the music is easy or intermediate in difficulty. Longer and more complex arpeggio pieces/studies are included at the end of the book.

This book is presented in three sections:

The first section will include the fundamental arpeggio forms and cover the two basic right-hand movements: *sympathetic* movement and *alternation*. Short exercises, easy pieces, arrangements and studies from existing guitar literature will be included so that each arpeggio form can be properly studied. *Simple* arpeggio forms will be combined to make *complex* arpeggio forms. The most commonly used arpeggio forms will be covered here.

At the end of the first section string crossing, arpeggio forms that skip strings, cross-over patterns, and sweeps are covered.

The second section will cover hundreds of the most important arpeggio forms with short examples of each using easy chords in the first position. All arpeggio examples from Giuliani's *120 Studies for Right-Hand Development* will be presented.

Next there is a section listing thirty *common arpeggio forms*. The common arpeggio forms are presented in the same order in which they appear in the book. They are presented in the same format (with easy chords in the key of C) as Giuliani's *120 Studies*.

Part of this section will focus on the playing arpeggios with the Travis Pick or alternating bass (as developed by the great Chet Atkins and used by many contemporary fingerstyle players today). There is a list of some common Travis Pick patterns comparing the rotating bass and alternating bass patterns.

The last section part of this section gives you some musical examples using the Travis Pick.

The third section will feature arpeggio music of various styles. There are arrangements, original compositions and selections from the classic guitar literature. The music is more difficult and includes some of the great arpeggio pieces of all time.

Acknowledgments

A special thanks to talented guitar composer Larry Long of Knoxville, TN for writing several pieces for the book. Larry has been playing guitar since 1958 and been teaching since 1962 at the University of Tennessee and in his own studio. In 1994 he was named to Who's Who Among America's Teachers. Thanks to Bill Bay and Mel Bay Publications for their support. Last but not least, loving thanks to my wife Rhonda.

The album, *True Blue* by Richard L.Matteson is available in cassette from the author. Several songs from *True Blue* appear in this book.

Tablature Explanation

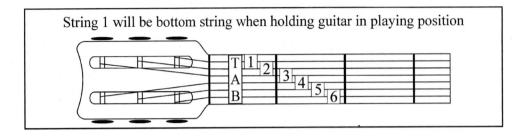

String 1 will be bottom string when holding guitar in playing position

Tablature: The six lines represent the six guitar strings. The numbers represent the frets.

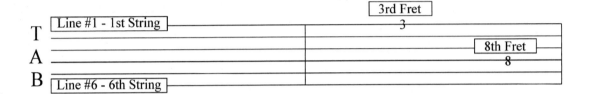

The Bend: Play the note and bend it up a whole step.

The Slide: Play the first note and slide up or down to the second note. The second note is not struck.

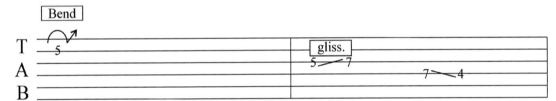

The Hammer-On: Play the lower note. Then, sound the higher note with another left-hand finger.

The Pull-Off: Play the higher note. Then, pull your left-hand finger off, sounding the second note.

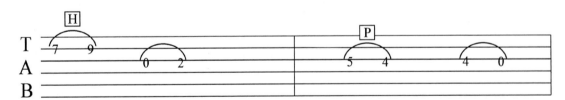

Vibrato: The string is vibrated rapidly by the left-hand finger(s).

Keynote: The note that names the key or scale is circled.

Glossary of Terms, Definitions and Basic Concepts

If you come across a word or term you don't understand, simply refer back to this page. Most of the terms in this book will be defined when they are first used.

The left-hand fingers

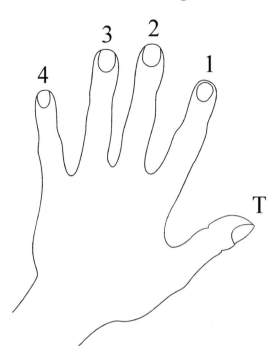

The right-hand fingers

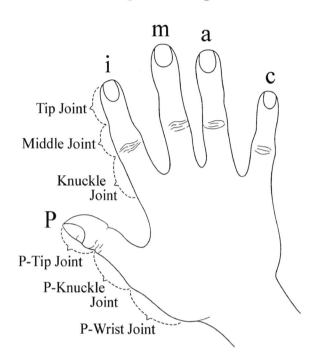

Glossary

__a__ - The third finger from the thumb on the right hand next to the pinky finger. See labels above.

Active finger - any finger that is being used to play an arpeggio form.

Alberti Bass - The name is derived from the Venetian composer Domenico Alberti (1710-1740) who created a pattern of chord notes in the bass voice as an accompaniment. The Alberti bass is similar to the Travis Pick or alternating- style bass parts found in guitar music today.

Alternation - occurs when a finger (or fingers) flexes at the same time another finger (or fingers) extends.

Alternating bass - is a pattern of chord notes played to accompany a melody or arpeggio piece usually with the thumb (**p**). A typical alternating bass would be between the root and fifth of a chord on the 6th, 5th or 4th strings (the bass strings).

Alternation arpeggios - are arpeggios that have one alternation (a finger flexes while another finger extends).

Arpeggio - from the Italian word arpa, "the harp." Arpeggio means playing a "broken chord" or the notes of a chord one after another (in succession) instead of at the same time (simultaneously). Also called a finger "roll."

Arpeggiate - to "roll" the chord quickly. On the guitar this roll usually starts on the bass strings with the thumb to the treble strings with the fingers. A wavy vertical line before a chord indicates the chord should be arpeggiated.

Arpeggio forms - a right-hand finger pattern. For example, **p, i, m** is an arpeggio form.

Arpeggios with __p__ - An arpeggio that uses the thumb (**p**).

Arpeggios without __p__ - An arpeggio without the thumb. For example, **a, m, i**.

Backward roll - fingers play from the treble strings toward the bass strings: **p, m, i** or **p, a, m, i**.

Backward-Forward roll - is a finger pattern from treble to bass and back to treble. For example **p, a, m, i, m, a**.

Bass strings - Typically the bass strings are the wound strings and are usually played with the thumb (**p**). Bass strings on a classic guitar are the 4th, 5th and 6th strings. On a steel-string acoustic guitar the 3rd string is usually wound and would also be a bass string. Occasionally the thumb plays strings other than the bass strings, just as the fingers may play on the bass strings, especially in scale passages.

c - "chico" or the small (pinky) finger on the right hand.

Chord - is three or more consecutive thirds (the 1st, 3rd and 5th notes of the scale) and/or their octaves which are sounded simultaneously or rapid succession (an arpeggio).

Chord progression - The order of the chords in a song or piece.

Complex arpeggios - The combining of two or more simple arpeggio forms.

Cross-over arpeggios - An arpeggio that uses a right-hand pattern where one of the fingers plays out of it's natural position (crosses over). For example, **a** plays the 2nd string then **m** crosses over to play the 1st string and **a** plays the 2nd string.

Cross-string arpeggios - are scales played on three or more string with a right-hand arpeggio pattern (similar to cross-string trills).

Extend (extension) - to use the extensor muscles to move the fingers or the thumb outward from a flexed position (after playing a string) so that the finger or thumb is ready to play again.

Finger roll - or roll is an arpeggio pattern played with the fingers and may also include the thumb. One derivation is from "banjo rolls."

Finger sweeps - Exercises used to develop the muscular coordination needed to play rapid arpeggios. Sweets involve strumming more then one string with a right-hand finger or the thumb.

Fingering - refers to which right-hand (**p, i, m, a**) and left-hand (1, 2, 3, 4) fingers are used to play a piece.

Flex; (flexion) - Use of the flexor muscles to move the fingers or thumb inward toward the palm.

Follow-through - the release of tension after muscular exertion, allowing the finger or thumb to move past the string instead of applying counterproductive tension to stop the movement.

Forward rolls - are arpeggios that go from bass toward the treble strings: **p, i, m** or **p, i, m, a**.

Free stroke - After sounding a string, the finger or thumb moves freely over the next adjacent string(s). Free stroke (tirando) is the most common stroke used to play arpeggios allowing the adjacent strings to ring like a harp.

Inactive finger - a finger that is not being used to play an arpeggio form, such as the **a** finger in the **p, i, m** arpeggio.

Left-hand fingers - are designated by numbers; 1(index), 2(middle), 3(ring), 4(pinky). Occasionally the left-hand thumb (T) is used to fret strings. It is employed for unusual stretches as in cello technique or to wrap around the neck to fret bass notes by some jazz and rock guitarists.

m - the middle finger (media) of the right hand.

M.M. - Metronome marking shows the number of beats per minute (tempo) that a piece should be played.

Muscular exertion - is the muscular energy required to perform a specific muscular function.

Muting - a technique of the right or left hand to prevent or stop the vibration of the string(s). Used in the traditional Travis picking method. See also palm muting.

p - the thumb (pulgar) of the right hand.

Palm muting - is resting the base of the right-hand palm against the bass string at the bridge so that the bass strings produce a produce a percussive staccato timbre. Used in traditional Travis picking and Chet Atkins style picking as well as in rock or classical music.

Planting - is resting the flesh of the right-hand fingertips against the strings. As the fingertips touch the strings there is a momentary pause and dampening of the string.

Prepared stoke - is another term for planting.

Rest stroke - After playing a string the right-hand finger or thumb comes to rest on the next adjacent string. The rest stroke (appoyando), generally a louder and more powerful stroke, is sometimes used to bring out the melody line in arpeggio pieces or to accentuate a melodic bass part in an arpeggio section.

Roll - is a right-hand arpeggio form.

Rotating bass - is a type of alternating bass where the thumb alternation is limited to two chord notes usually the root and fifth. This bass technique is frequently used in Travis Picking.

Right-hand fingers - the letters **p, i, m, a, c** have been underlined when used in text to prevent confusion with letters the alphabet. Right-hand fingers without a comma in between (with a dash) indicate that the fingers play simultaneously (**p, i-m**).

Scale - is a set of notes grouped around a central note or keynote. The western system of music uses a system of scales and modes arranging the first seven letters of the alphabet into intervals of half-steps (1 fret) and whole steps (2 frets).

Short chord - is really an interval because it is missing one of the three consecutive thirds that make up a chord. A short chord implies a chord.

Simple arpeggios - are arpeggios that don't require any alternation of the right hand fingers. When grouped together they are called *complex arpeggios*.

Skipping (string) arpeggios - are arpeggio patterns where adjacent right-hand fingers skip over one or more strings. For example, **i** plays the 4th string and **m** plays the 2nd string.

String crossing - is the movement of the right hand from the elbow required when shifting the fingers to play on different strings. For example play **p, i, m** on 4th, 3rd & 2nd strings, then shift to play **p,i,m** on the 3rd, 2nd & 1st strings. The right hand would need to shift the distance of one string to keep the same alignment.

Sweep - are defined as playing two or more strings with one finger or the thumb. This is usually accomplished by sweeping up (from the trebles to the basses) with the **a** or **m** fingers or sweeping down (from the basses to the trebles) with the thumb.

*Sweeps with **p*** - using the right hand thumb (**p**) to sweep down across the strings. For example, arpeggiating the six strings (from basses to treble) **p, p, p, i, m, a**.

*Sweeps with **a*** - using the right-hand **a** finger to sweep upward across the strings.

Sympathetic movement - using the natural muscular pull to move two or more right-hand fingers in the same direction (forward or backward) on successive notes.

Sympathetic movement arpeggios - use movement in the same direction.

Travis Pick - is attributed to legendary guitarist Merle Travis and popularized by the great Chet Atkins and others. The original formula used by Travis was a bass strum, alternate bass, strum pattern played entirely by the thumb (as the palm muted the bass strings) while the fingers played melody and harmony parts on the treble strings. Frequently the strum has been replaced by a different bass note making the pattern: bass, bass 2, alternate bass, bass 2. Other popular patterns include the rotating bass or alternation between two bass notes.

Treble strings - refer to the 1st, 2nd and 3rd string or unwound strings (nylon strings on a classic guitar). On an acoustic steel-string guitar the 3rd string is usually wound.

Tremelo - refers to the repeated playing of a single note in rapid succession. On the guitar common tremolo patterns are the two finger **p, m, i** the three finger **p, a, m, i** and the four finger **p, i, a, m, i** (also **p, c, a, m, i**).

Basic Right–Hand Movement

The basic right hand movement for playing arpeggios is this: *When the thumb (**p**) plays - the fingers move out* (getting in position to play) *and when the fingers play - the thumb moves out* (getting back in position to play).

This is a form of alternation between the fingers and the thumb. Thumb in fingers out; fingers in - thumb out.

Note: Don't forget to move the right-hand pinkie finger (**c**) along with the third finger (**a**) in all the arpeggio forms and exercises. Normally the short finger (**c**) is not used to play arpeggios and is flexed along with the third finger (**a**). In general, inactive fingers (a finger not being used to play in the arpeggio form) move along with active fingers. Not moving an inactive finger will inhibit the movement of an active finger.

Exercise 1: Basic Right-Hand Movement

Step 1 Make a fist with your right hand, keeping your wrist straight. Pull your right thumb (**p**) out (extend fully) away from your index as if you were getting ready to play your thumb (**p**). See illustration 1 below.

Step 2 Now throw your fingers out (extend) so that your fingers and hand are straight and at the same time move your thumb in (flex) as if you were playing your thumb. Let your thumb (**p**) follow through until it rests underneath your straightened fingers. See illustration 2 below.

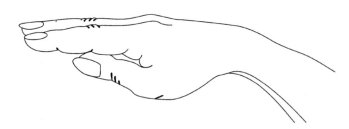

Step 3 Now flex your fingers back to your palm (making a loose fist) *at the same time* extend your thumb back out. Your hand should now be back in starting position (step 1). Repeat this exercise until it becomes automatic and comfortable. Visualize that you are playing guitar.

Basic Right–Hand Movement

More Exercises; Playing the Basic Movement on the Guitar

Now that you understand the basic right-hand movement, here's an exercise to develop the correct movement of the right-hand fingers when playing an arpeggio.

Basic Right-Hand Movement Exercises 2 - While you are sitting down, place your right-hand thumb on your right knee. Keep your wrist slightly arched (don't rest your wrist on your knee - keep it several inches away from your knee/leg) as if you are playing the guitar. Extend your fingers out and gently scratch (flex them) across the top of your knee (or pants) with **i** and **m**.

Remember to move your inactive fingers (**a** and **c**) along with **i** and **m**. Follow through until your finger tips lightly touch palm. Make most of the flexion with your tip joints and middle joints.

Notice that your knuckle joint moves down (flexes) slightly. One of the problems to watch out for is making sure there is a slight downward movement of knuckle joints - if the *knuckle joints move up at all when playing arpeggios your finger movements are wrong*. Try arching you wrist more or following through more.

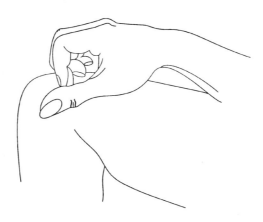

Basic Right-Hand Movement - Playing the Guitar, Exercises 3.

After practicing Exercise 2 on your knee, you are ready to play it on the guitar. The three exercises below are played on open strings. Try to exaggerate the follow through after playing the string(s) to develop a powerful tone.

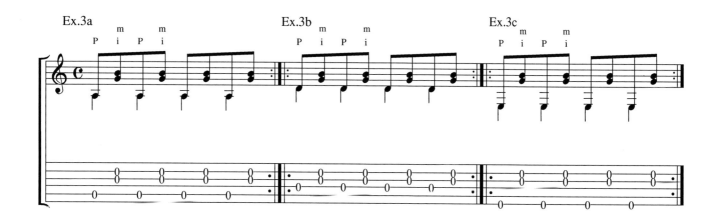

Basic Right–Hand Movement

Exercises for Guitar (**p, i-m**)

Here are some short music exercises to help develop your basic hand movement. In Ex. 4 the treble part (played with **i-m**) remains open while **p** plays a G major scale pattern. Ex. 5 has **p** playing the open 6th string while the melody is played with the fingers. Go slowly with Ex. 6, the left hand is tricky. Ex. 7, watch the change in the bass between C major and Am.

Are the third (**a**) and fourth (**c**) fingers of your right hand relaxed and flexing along with **i-m**? Are you still focused on the correct hand movement?

Ex.4 Scale in Bass

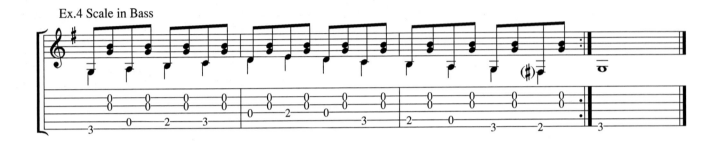

Ex.5 Steady Bass

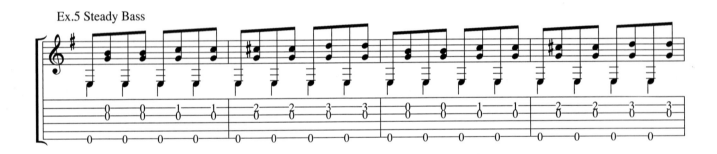

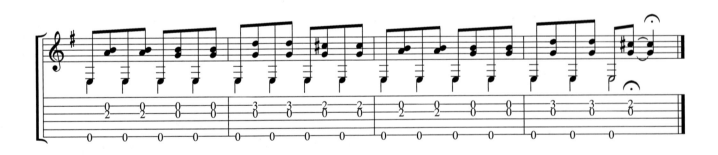

Ex.6 Jazz Turnaround

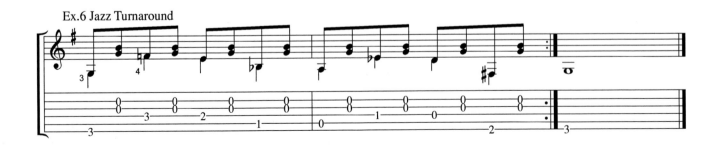

Ex.7 In Dust We Trust

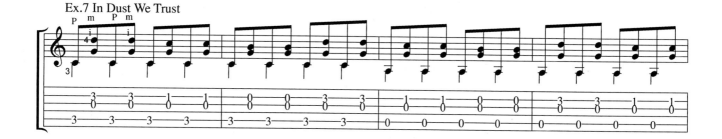

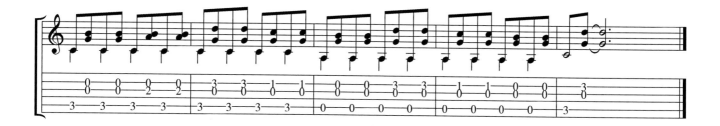

Simple Arpeggio Forms

Sympathetic Arpeggio Forms - Forward Rolls

In *simple arpeggio forms* the fingers move in one direction (either forward - **p, i, m** or backward - **p, m, i**) and no alternation (moving in opposite directions) between fingers occur. When one finger plays it pulls the other fingers in the same direction-the pull of one finger on another is called *sympathetic movement*. Your fingers move more quickly in the same direction because they use sympathetic movement; the natural pull of the fingers with one another.

The p, i, m Arpeggio

When you've developed and have some security with the basic hand movement and the **p,i-m** exercises you're ready for your first arpeggio. Approach the **p, i, m** arpeggio the same way you did with the basic hand exercises.

First play **p**, then move **i-m** out and prepare them on the 3rd and 2nd strings. The only difference is: *When you play **i** on the 3rd string, **m** will be pulled sympathetically into the 2nd string.* Immediately flex **m** and follow through, playing the 2nd string.

Carefully watch your **i, m** fingers when playing the open string exercises below. Make sure **i** and **m** are moving in the same direction.

Preparing one or more fingers on the string (prepared stroke) is called planting. If you learn how to plant well, something might grow!

Open - String **p, i, m** Arpeggio Exercises

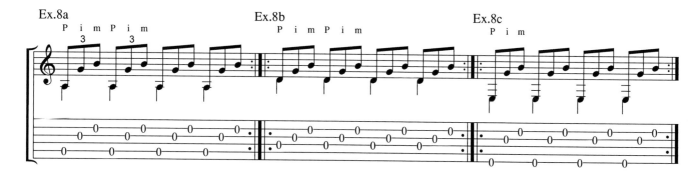

Simple Arpeggio Forms

Forward Rolls; Exercises for the **p, i, m** Arpeggio

P i m Ex.9 Walkin' the Elephant

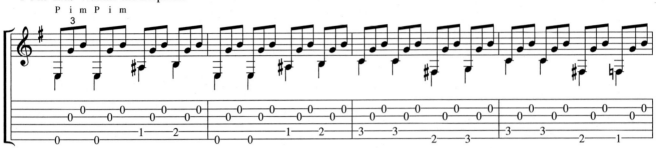

P i m Ex.10 Love Song

P i m Ex.11 Chanson

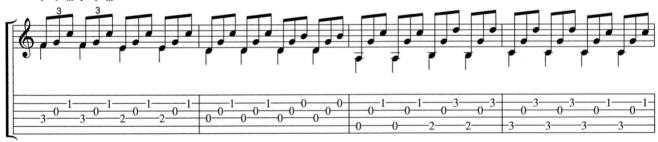

Simple Arpeggio Forms

Forward Rolls; More Exercises for the **p, i, m** Arpeggio

Simple Arpeggio Forms
Forward Rolls; Study for the **p, i, m** Arpeggio

P i m Ex.14 Study in Em

Simple Arpeggio Forms
Forward Rolls; Basic Right-Hand Movement, p,i-a Form

The **p,i-a** basic right-hand form is the same as **p,i-m** form except you substitute the a finger for **m**. When you play **p,i-a** the inactive **m** finger is slightly elevated and moves with **i-a**. Be sure to move the other inactive finger **c** along with **a**.

Basic Right Hand Movement Exercises p,i-a

P i a Basic Right Hand

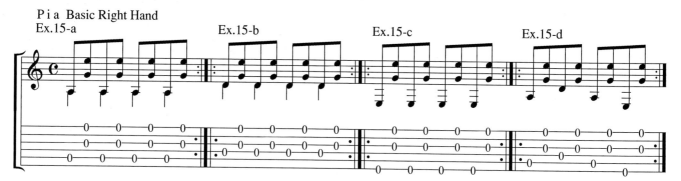

After you develop a secure right hand movement with open strings try music exercises 16-18.

Ex.16 Down in the Delta

Ex.17 Leyenda

17

Simple Arpeggio Forms

Basic Right-Hand Movement, **p,i,a** Form; **p,i,a** Forward Roll

Ex.18 Blues in my Walking Shoes

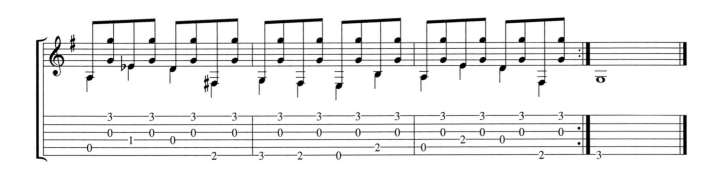

The p,i,a arpeggio

The **p,i,a** arpeggio is the same as **p,i-a** basic form except you play the **i** finger first letting sympathetic movement pull the **a** finger gently into the first string. Since **i** and **a** are not adjacent fingers there is less pull sympathetically than most arpeggios. When you play **p,i,a** the inactive **m** finger is slightly elevated and moves with **i-a**. Once again, be sure to move the other inactive finger **c** along with **a**.

Ex.19-a   Ex.19-b   Ex.19-c   Ex.19-d

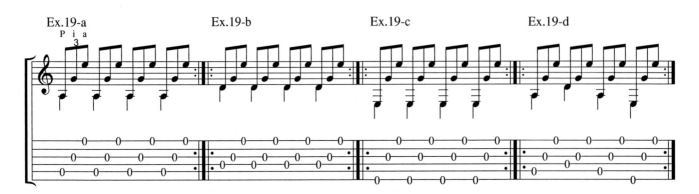

Simple Arpeggio Forms

p.i.a Forward Roll Exercises

Here (and on the next page) are three more **p.i.a** exercises. You can also go back and do the **p.i-a** exercises 16-18 if you need more **p.i.a** studies.

Ex.20 Somber Mood

P i a Ex. 21 Sweet Melissa

Simple Arpeggio Forms

Forward Roll **p.i.a** Exercise. Basic Right-Hand Movement Form **p.m-a**

Pi a Ex.22 Blues in the Night

Basic Movement **p.m-a**

The **p.m-a** basic right-hand movement will prepare you for the **p.m.a** arpeggio. The **p.m.a** arpeggio is infrequently used by itself (usually **p.i.m** is used). However, the development of this form is important for the **p.i.m.a** arpeggio so **p.m.a** and its basic movement **p.m-a** are included. Here are the open string exercises.

P, m-a Basic Movement
Ex.23-a   Ex.23-b   Ex.23-c   Ex.23-d

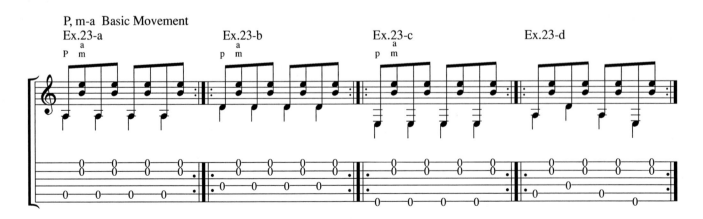

Simple Arpeggio Forms

Basic Movement **p,m-a** Exercises. The **p,m,a** Arpeggio: Open Strings

Ex.24 Runnin' Thru the Rye

The p,m,a Arpeggio

The **p,m,a** arpeggio is important for developing the **a** finger to use in the **p,i,m,a** forward roll. Since the **a** finger is one of the weak (less independent) fingers in the hand, there will be more sympathetic pull on **a** when playing the adjacent **m** finger.

Place both **m** and **a** on the 2nd and 1st strings as if playing the previous **p,m-a** basic movement exercises (23-25). Play **m**. Notice that **a** is pulled into the 1st string when **m** follows through. As you feel **a** being pulled into the 1st string play **a**. Remember to flex the inactive fingers **i** and **c**. Do the open string exercises below slowly at first.

Ex.26 A

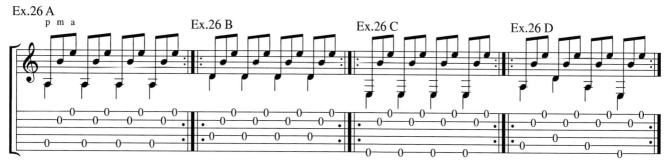

Simple Arpeggio Forms

The **p.m.a** Arpeggio Exercises

Simple Arpeggio Forms
Basic Movement **p.i-m-a** Open and Other Exercises

The **p.i-m-a** basic movement form develops coordination for the important **p.i.m.a** arpeggio. Emphasize extending the **a** finger slightly more than **m** and **i** when moving the fingers to the strings.

Ex.29 A   Ex.29 B   Ex.29 C   Ex.29 D

Ex.30 Minor Mood

Ex.31 Like a Warm Breeze

Ex.32 Fandango

Simple Arpeggio Forms
The **p.i.m.a** Arpeggio: Open Strings and Exercises

The **p.i.m.a** arpeggio form is approached in the same way as the **p.i-m-a** basic form. Prepare the fingers (**i-m-a**) on the treble string after playing **p** on the bass strings. Emphasize extending the **a** finger slightly more that **i-m**. This will make your finger placement easier.

Simple Arpeggio Forms
The **p.i.m.a** Arpeggio

Simple Arpeggio Forms
The p.i.m.a Arpeggio

Simple Arpeggio Forms

Sympathetic Movement for Backward Rolls. The p,m,i Arpeggio

The backward rolls (**p.m.i**) (**p.a.i**) (**p.a.m**) (**p.a.m.i**) and tremolo (**p.m.i**) (**p.a.m.i**) are simple arpeggio forms (the fingers move in the same direction with no alternation) and use sympathetic movement.

Because of the natural condition of the fingers, the backward rolls are easier and faster. Put your right hand in playing position with your wrist slightly arched and completely relax your fingers and thumb. Notice how your index extends naturally more than your other fingers and that your **m** finger extends slightly more than **a**. See illustration 4 below.

The difficulty with forward rolls is the extension of the **a** finger (which moves out first). Even with the **p.i.m** arpeggio, the **a** finger must be extended and flexed as an inactive finger. However, when playing the backward rolls the fingers extended in a similar position as your relaxed fingers. The **i** finger extends first, then **m**, and lastly **a** (with the inactive finger **c**).

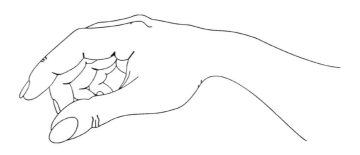

The **p.m.i** Arpeggio

To play the **p.m.i** arpeggio you may review the basic hand movement and **p.i-m** exercises. Remember that **i** extends out first slightly and is pulled sympathetically by **m**. Make sure both fingers move together *in the same direction*.

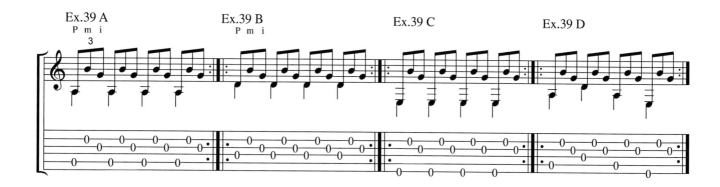

Simple Arpeggio Forms

The **p.m.i** Arpeggio; Study

Ex.40 Pop Song

Simple Arpeggio Forms

The **p.m.i** Arpeggio; More Studies

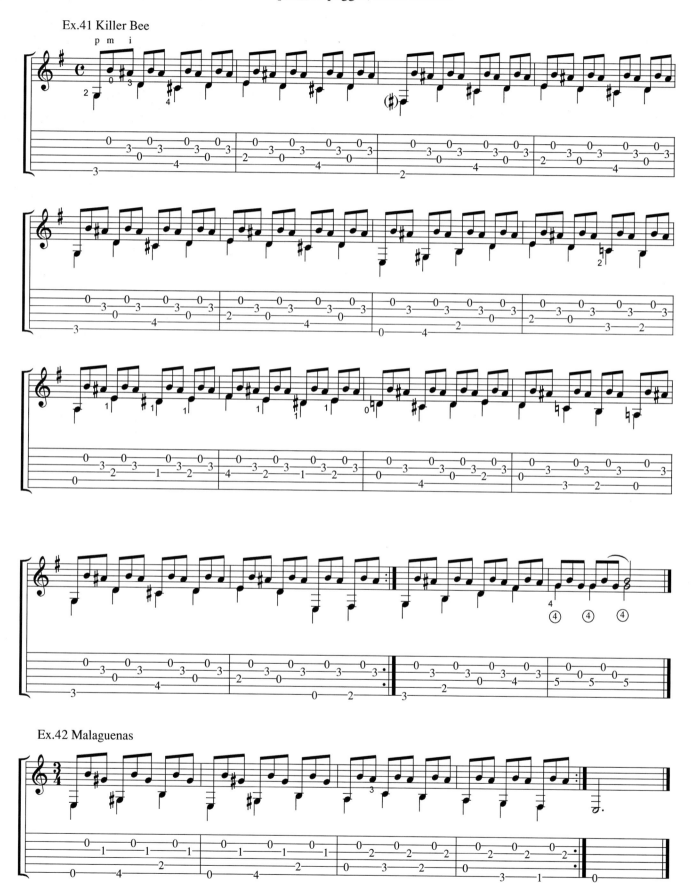

Ex.41 Killer Bee

Ex.42 Malaguenas

Simple Arpeggio Forms

The **p.m.i** Arpeggio; Last Studies

Ex.43 Child's Play

Ex. 44 Study on Two Strings

Fandango de Huelva

Traditional Flamenco; Arr. by R. Matteson

p,m,i Study

Simple Arpeggio Forms

Intro to the **p.a.i** Arpeggio; Open Strings; Exercises

The **p.a.i** arpeggio is similar to the **p.m.i** arpeggio: both are backward rolls and use sympathetic movement. The **p.a.i** arpeggio is good for developing strength and coordination in the weaker **a** finger. When extending **a**, make sure **i** and then **m** (an inactive finger) extend first and that **m** and **c** flex when **a** plays.

Review the **p.i-a** and **p.i.a** exercises (reverse the arpeggio to **p.a.i**) for extra practice pieces.

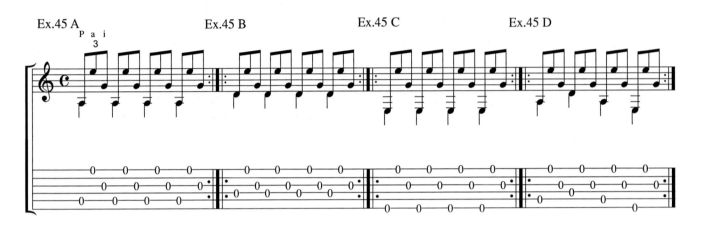

Ex.45 A   Ex.45 B   Ex.45 C   Ex.45 D

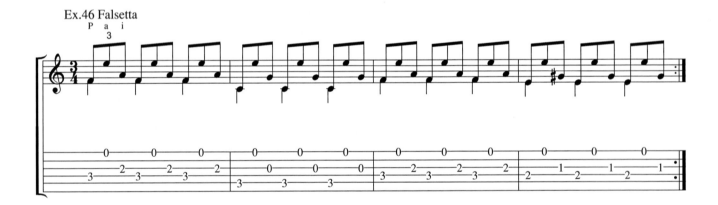

Ex.46 Falsetta

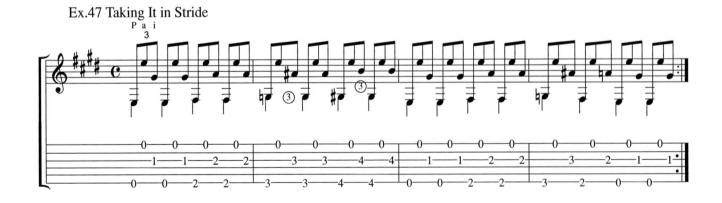

Ex.47 Taking It in Stride

Simple Arpeggio Forms

The **p,a,i** Arpeggio; Intro to **p,a,m**

Ex.48 Nothing But the Blues

The **p,a,m** Arpeggio

The **p,a,m** arpeggio is infrequently used (usually **p,m,i**) but will prepare you for the **p,a,m,i** arpeggio and tremolo (also **p,a,m,i**).

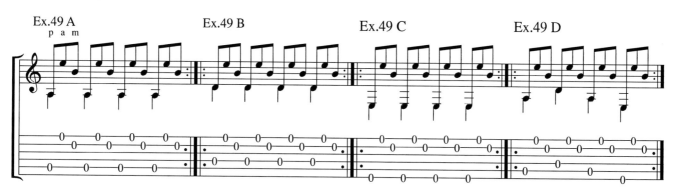

Ex.49 A   Ex.49 B   Ex.49 C   Ex.49 D

Simple Arpeggio Forms
The **p.a.m** Arpeggio

Ex.50 Rockin'

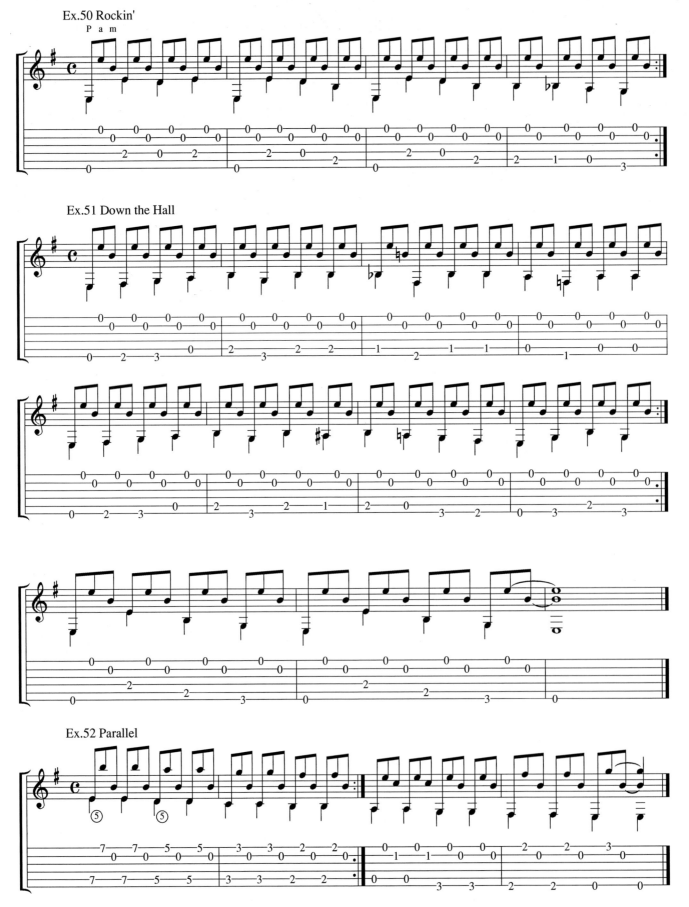

Ex.51 Down the Hall

Ex.52 Parallel

Simple Arpeggio Forms
The **p.a.m.i** Arpeggio Intro and Exercises

The **p.a.m.i** arpeggio form is widely used because it is the same form used in tremolo (where the **a.m.i** fingers play on the string). Played correctly the **p.a.m.i** arpeggio will look like a wave with the **a** finger leading **m**, then **i**.

The **p.a.m.i** arpeggio is the last sympathetic movement arpeggio form.

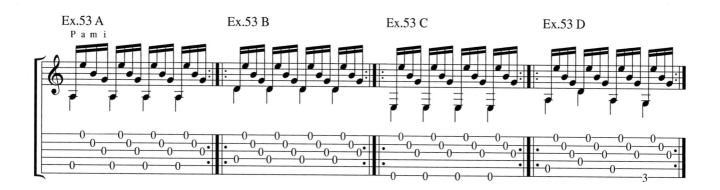

Ex.53 A   Ex.53 B   Ex.53 C   Ex.53 D

P a m i

Ex.54 Evening

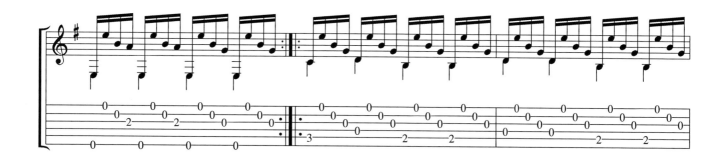

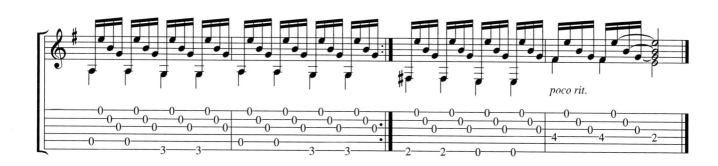

poco rit.

35

Simple Arpeggio Forms

The p.a.m.i Arpeggio Exercises

Ex.55 True Blue

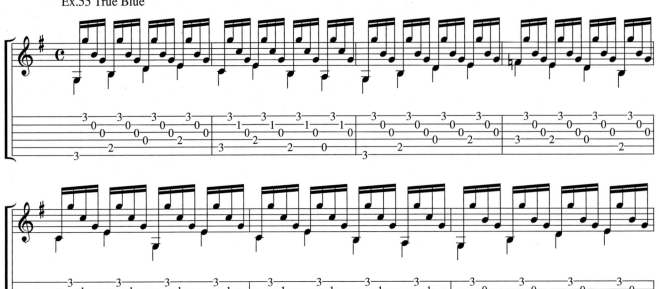

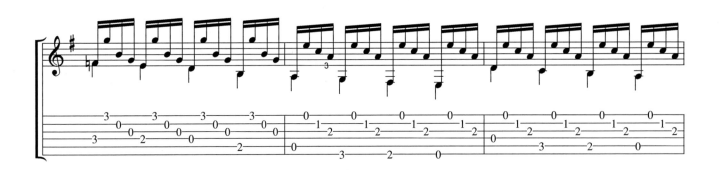

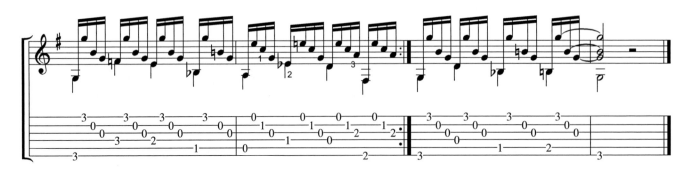

Ex.56 Sixties Riff

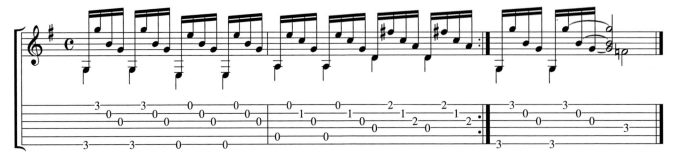

Simple Arpeggio Forms
The **p.a.m.i** Arpeggio Exercises

Ex.57 Fandango de Huelva II

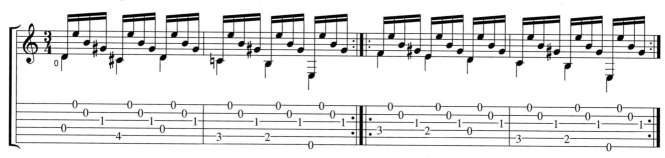

Ex.58 Flat Seventh

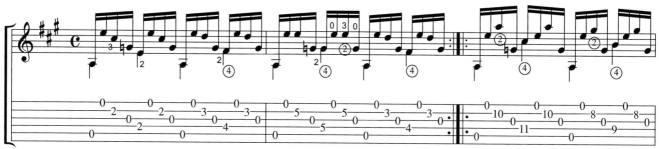

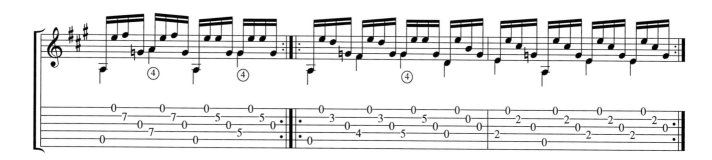

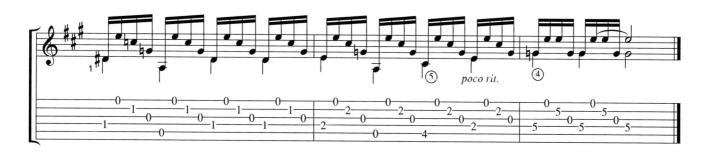

Simple Arpeggio Forms
Tremolo Introduction; **p.m.i** Tremolo Exercises

Tremolo on the guitar is defined as repeatedly playing one note at a fast tempo. For the fingerstyle or classic guitarist, the thumb usually plays the bass while the fingers play the tremolo.

The main types of tremolo are **p.m.i** (two note) and **p.a.m.i** (three note). Some flamenco guitarists use a four note tremolo played **p.i.a.m.i** (that uses one alternation) or **p.c.a.m.i**. The four note tremolo will not be covered here, but you may try it on any tremolo study. Other tremolos of longer duration are also possible - **p.i.m.a.m.i**.

Until this point in the book, your finger position (**i** plays 3rd string, **m** plays 2nd string, **a** plays 1st string) has remained constant. To play tremolo on the first string your hand should shift from the elbow down one string as if **m** was playing the first string. This is called string crossing and is covered later on page 64.

The **p.m.i** Tremolo

The **p.m.i** tremolo should be played the same as **p.m.i** arpeggio. When playing on the first string, shift your hand down (from the elbow keeping your finger position the same) one string.

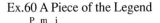

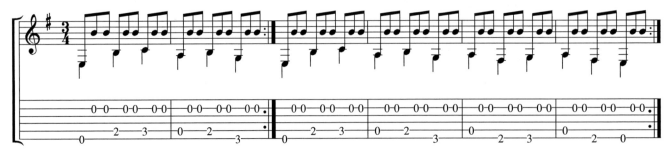

38

Simple Arpeggio Forms

p.m.i Tremolo Exercises

Ex.61 Dawn

Ex.62 Study in Dm

Simple Arpeggio Forms

p.a.m.i Tremolo Introductio; Exercises

The **p.a.m.i** one of the most striking and beautiful arpeggio forms played on the guitar.

The **p.a.m.i** tremolo is the same movement form as the **p.a.m.i** arpeggio. When playing on the first string (Ex. 64-A), shift your hand down (from the elbow, keeping your hand position the same) one string.

Simple Arpeggio Forms

p.a.m.i Tremolo Exercises

In Ex. 66 *Blues Boogie* keep your 3rd left hand finger on the 2nd string 3rd fret (D note) throughout. Ex. 67 *Twinkle Melody* is an example of a melody played in the treble part with the fingers.

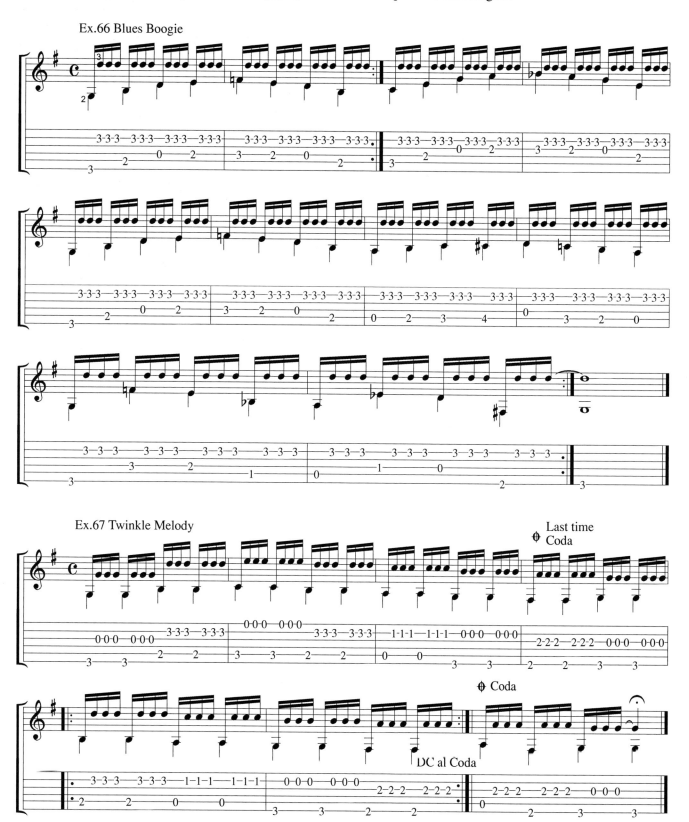

Simple Arpeggio Forms
p,a,m,i Tremolo Exercises

Ex.68 Malaguenas

Ex.69 Climbing the Ladder

Ex. 70 Soleares Falsetta

Complex Arpeggio Forms

Alternation-Basic Concepts; Exercises Without the Guitar

Alternation occurs when fingers *move in opposite directions*. Arpeggios that use alternation are called complex arpeggios because they combine a simple arpeggio form (**p,i,m**) that uses sympathetic movement with an alternation (**p,i,m,i**).

The two fundamental alternations used by the right-hand are **i** alternating with **m** (the inactive fingers **a** and **c** move with **m**) and **m** (with the inactive finger **i**) alternating with the more difficult finger **a** (with the inactive finger **c**).

Below are two important exercises to develop coordination and speed for right-hand alternation.

Exercises 1: Alternation of i and m

Hold your right hand out and put it in playing position with your wrist slightly arched (see illustration 5 below). Keep your thumb relaxed the entire exercise. *Don't move your knuckle joints*, only your middle and tip joints. Flex and extend fully to give the muscles a maximum workout.

Step 1 - Extend your fingers out until they are straight.

Step 2 - Flex **i** (your index) only. Keep your knuckle joint straight with your other fingers.

Step 3 - Extend **i** (straight out) and *at the same time* flex **m-a-c**. Don't move your knuckle joints only your middle joints and tip joints.

Step 4 - Flex **i** and extend **m-a-c** at the same time. Repeat Step 3 and 4 as necessary.

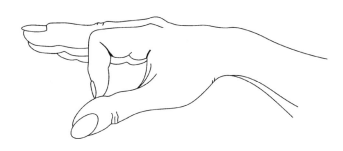

Exercises 2: Alternation of m and a

Position your hand like Ex. 1. Keep your thumb relaxed and your knuckle joints in playing position. Don't move your knuckle joints.

Step 1 - Extend your fingers straight out.

Step 2 - Flex **i** and **m** together, keep **a** and **c** straight.

Step 3 - Extend **i-m** and flex **a-c** at the same time.

Step 4 - Flex **a-c** and extend **i-m** at the same time. Repeat Step 3 and 4.

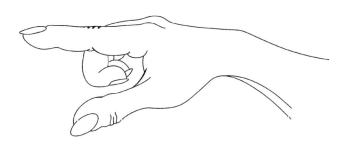

Complex Arpeggio Forms
Alternation; Exercises on the Guitar

Alternation is used to play scales and arpeggios. The fingers usually alternate on different strings when playing arpeggios, while they play on the same and different strings to play scales.

Alternation of **i,m** is the same movement form as **m,i** you just start with a different finger.

i,m and m,i Alternation

Place **i** (3rd string) and **m** (2nd string) on the strings as if you were using preparation to play **p,i-m**, only this time **p** will not be used. Flex **i**, playing the 3rd string open. Don't move the **m** finger, hold the **m** fingertip lightly against the 2nd string.

Now play **m**, *at the same time* extend **i** in the opposite direction and place **i** on the 3rd string. Look at your fingers: **m** along with the inactive fingers **a** and **c** are flexed while the **i** fingertip is touching the 3rd string ready to play.

Play **i**, at the same time extend **m** (along with **a,c**) and place **m** on the 2nd string. If you repeat the **i,m** alternation slowly many times emphasizing follow-through, you will develop good muscular coordination and a powerful sound.

Complex Arpeggio Forms
i,m and m,i Alternation; Exercises

Ex. 76 Pop Formula

Ex. 76 Pop Formula with Bass

Ex. 77 Variation on Pop Formula

Ex. 77 Variation with Bass

Ex. 78 Simple Melody

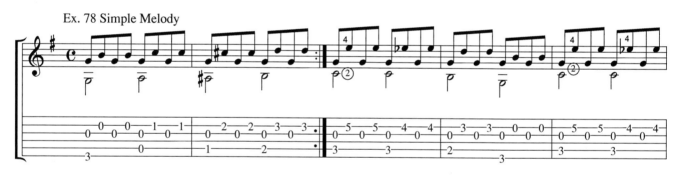

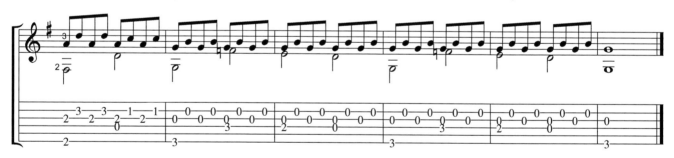

Ex. 79 AB Study

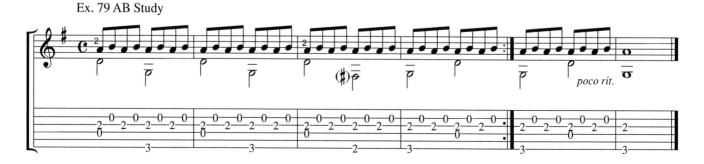

poco rit.

Complex Arpeggio Forms

i.a and a.i Alternation; Exercises

Play the **i.a** alternation the same as the **i.m** alternation. When playing the open string exercises, make sure the inactive fingers (**m** and **c**) move along with the **a** finger.

Ex. 80   Ex. 81A   Ex. 81B   Ex. 81C   Ex. 81D

Ex. 82   Ex. 83A   Ex. 83B   Ex. 83C   Ex. 84

Ex. 85 Mr. Bo

Ex. 86 Turnaround

Ex. 87 Study in C

Ode to Joy

by L. Beethoven; Arr. R. Matteson

Alternation **a,i** Alternation **m,i**; **p,i,m** Arpeggio

Complex Arpeggio Forms

m,a and **a,m** Alternation; Exercises

The **m,a** (and **a,m**) alternation is the most difficult alternation for the right hand. When playing the open string exercises, make sure the inactive finger **c** moves along with the **a** finger. The inactive finger **i** moves with **m**.

Complex Arpeggio Forms

Arpeggios without **p** Introduction; **i,m,a** Arpeggio Form

Arpeggios are also played without the thumb (**p**). In these arpeggios the fingers play the arpeggio pattern and **p** is free to play a bass part.

There are two distinct movement forms: the **i,m,a** arpeggio form and the **a,m,i** arpeggio form.

Look at this repeated pattern of **i,m,a**: (i,m,a,i,m,a,**i,m,a**,i,m,a). Now we will write out the **i,m,a** arpeggio but start with the **m** finger first: (m,a,i,m,a,i,**m,a,i**,m,a,i). The **m,a,i** arpeggio is the same movement form as the **i,m,a** it just *starts with a different finger.*

Now we will write out the **i,m,a** arpeggio but start with the **a** finger first: (a,i,m,a,i,m,**a,i,m**,a,i,m). The **a,i,m** arpeggio has the same finger movement as the **i,m,a** arpeggio form. Both the **m,a,i** and **a,i,m** arpeggios *are derivatives* of the **i,m,a** form.

The **i,m,a** forms and their derivatives are complex arpeggio forms. A complex arpeggio has at least one sympathetic movement (where two active fingers move in opposite directions) and one alternation (where two active fingers *move in opposite directions*).

Other complex finger patterns without **p** may be created from the basic **i,m,a** and **a,m,i** forms and their derivatives. The **i,m,a,m** or **a,m,i,m** arpeggios are two of thousands of possibilities. All complex arpeggios can be analyzed so that you can understand the basic sympathetic movement(s) and alternation(s).

The **i,m,a** Arpeggio Form

The **i,m,a** arpeggio is a complex arpeggio form. There is a sympathetic movement between **m,a** and alternation between **i,m**.

The easiest way to understand the movement form is to substitute **p** for **i**. This will be the **p,m,a** forward roll in Ex. 95 below. After reviewing the **p,m,a** movement replace **p** with **i** and play Ex. 96-A. This is the **i,m,a** arpeggio form.

Feel the sympathetic movement between **m,a**. In Ex. 96-B and 96-C a bass part played with the thumb has been added.

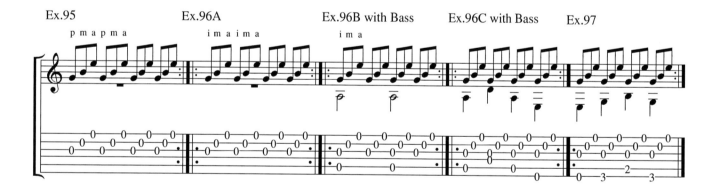

Complex Arpeggio Forms

Arpeggios without **p**; The **i,m,a** Arpeggio Form

m,a,i: An i,m,a Arpeggio Form Derivative

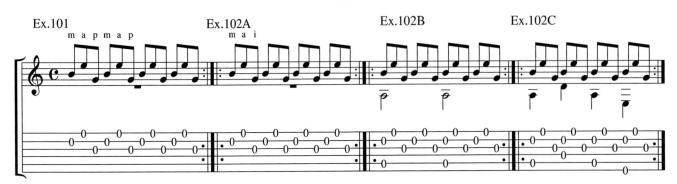

Back Up and Push

by R. Matteson; Based on a Traditional Fiddle Tune

i.m.a Study

Complex Arpeggio Forms

Arpeggios Without **p**; The **i.m.a** Arpeggio Form; **m.a.i** and **a.i.m**

The **a.i.m** arpeggio form is the most widely used derivative of the **i.m.a** forms because the highest note (melody note) is played first. In Ex. 107 *Study in Em*, the melody notes are played entirely with the **a** finger.

52

Complex Arpeggio Forms

Arpeggios Without **p**; The **a,m,i** Arpeggio Form

The **a,m,i** arpeggio form is the second fundamental arpeggio without **p**. The **a,m,i** arpeggio is a complex arpeggio with sympathetic movement between **a,m** and an alternation between **m,i**.

To understand the **a,m,i** form practice Ex.108 (the **p,a,m** form) in which **p** is substituted for **i**.

The **a,m,i** form has two derivatives: the **m,i,a** form and the **i,a,m** form. The **a,m,i** form is the most widely used because the highest note (melody note) is played first.

Study in Em

Attributed to F. Tarrega; and Fingered by R. Matteson

a.m.i Study

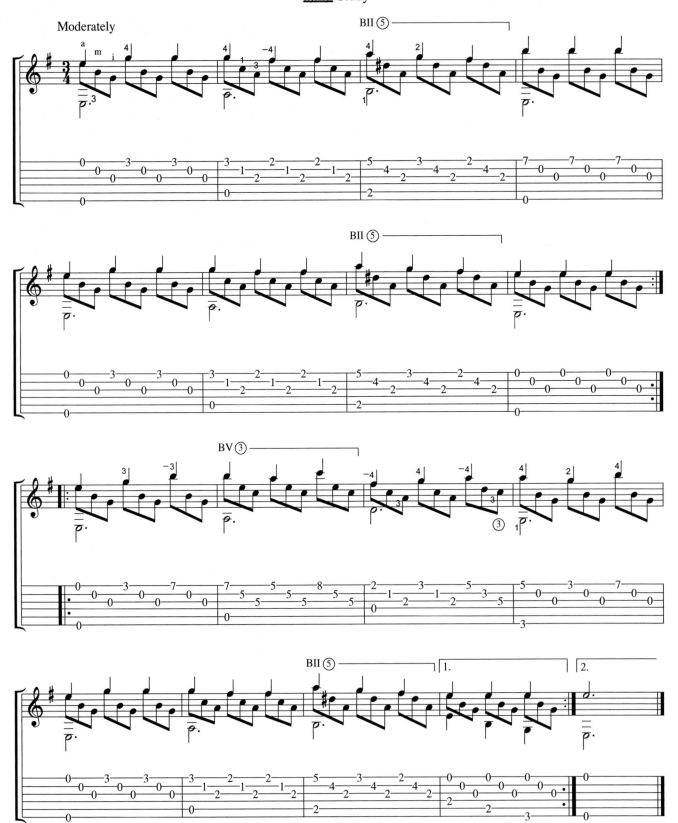

Complex Arpeggio Forms

Arpeggios Without **p**; The **a,m,i** Derivatives: **m,i,a** and **i,a,m**

Complex Arpeggio Forms

Arpeggios With **p**; The Forward-Backward Rolls; **p.i.m.i**

Complex arpeggios with **p** are arpeggio forms that have at least one sympathetic movement between active fingers, one alternation between active fingers and use **p** in the arpeggio form.

Forward-backward rolls (arpeggios) start from the bass string with **p** and go from the lowest treble (3rd string) toward the highest treble (1st string) and back.

The forward-backward rolls (**p.i.m.i**) (**p.i.a.i**) (**p.m.a.m**) (**p.i.m.a.m.i**) have two sympathetic movements and one alternation.

The **p.i.m.i** Arpeggio

The **p.i.m.i** arpeggio consists of one sympathetic movement (**p.i.m** forward roll), one alternation (after the **p.i.m** roll **i** must alternate with **m**) and another sympathetic movement (**m** follows through pulling **i**).

Remember to move the inactive fingers **a.c** along with **m**.

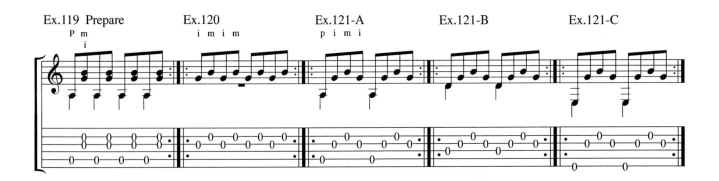

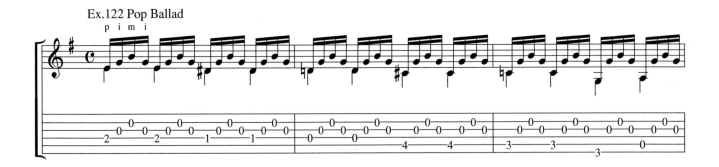

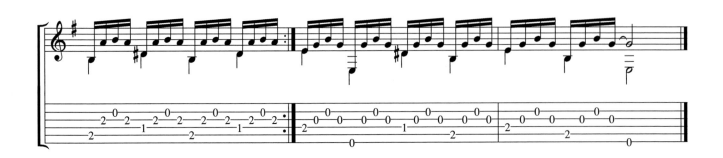

Freight Train–Two Variations

by Elizabeth Cotton; Arr. R. Matteson

a,m,i and **p,i,m,i** Study

Complex Arpeggio Forms

Arpeggios With **p**; The Forward-Backward Rolls; **p,i,a,i** and **p,m,a,m**

Complex Arpeggio Forms

Arpeggios With **p**; The Forward-Backward Rolls; **p.i.m.a.m.i**

    The **p.i.m.a.m.i** arpeggio consists of one sympathetic movement (**p.i.m.a** forward roll), one alternation (after the **p.i.m.a** roll, **m.i** must alternate with **a**) and another sympathetic movement (**a** follows through pulling **m** and then **i**).

    Remember to move the inactive finger **c** along with **a**.

The House of the Rising Sun

Traditional; Arranged by R. Matteson

p.i.m.a.m.i Study

Complex Arpeggio Forms

Arpeggios With **p**; The Forward-Backward Rolls; **p.m.i.m**

Complex arpeggios with **p** are arpeggio forms that have at least one sympathetic movement between active fingers, one alternation between active fingers and use **p** in the arpeggio form.

Backward-forward rolls (arpeggios) start from the bass strings with **p** and go from highest treble (1st string) toward the lowest treble (3rd string) and back.

The backward-forward rolls (**p.m.i.m**) (**p.a.i.a**) (**p.a.m.a**) (**p.a.m.i.m.a**) have two sympathetic movements and one alternation.

The **p.m.i.m** Arpeggio

The **p.m.i.m** arpeggio consists of one sympathetic movement (**p.m.i** backward roll), one alternation (after the **p.m.i** roll, **m** must alternate with **i**) and another sympathetic movement (**i** follows through pulling **m**).

Remember to move the inactive fingers **a.c** along with **m**.

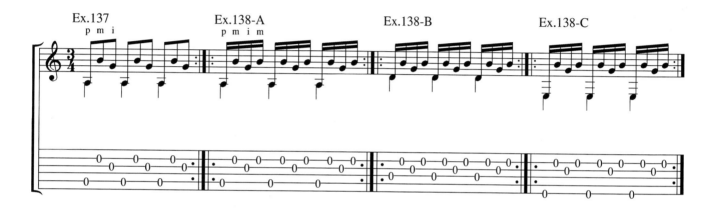

61

Complex Arpeggio Forms

Arpeggios With **p**; The Backward-Forward Rolls; **p.a.i.a** and **p.a.m.a**

The backward-forward rolls **p.a.i.a** and **p.a.m.a** have two sympathetic movements and one alternation. The **p.a.m.a** roll is usually played **p.m.i.m** but is included here to help develop alternation between **m.a**.

62

Complex Arpeggio Forms

Arpeggios With **p**; The Backward-Forward Rolls; **p.a.m.i.m.a**

The backward-forward roll **p.a.m.i.m.a** has two sympathetic movements and one alternation.

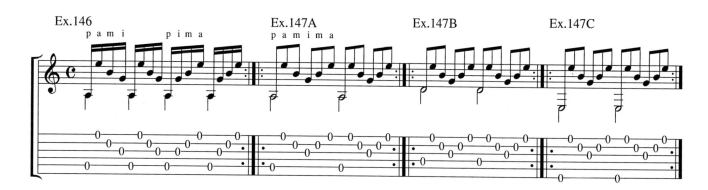

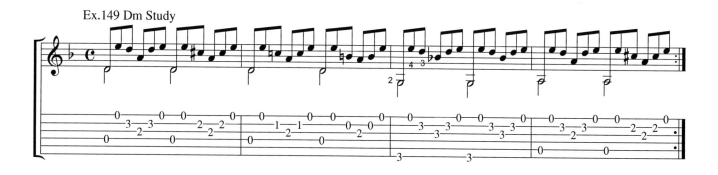

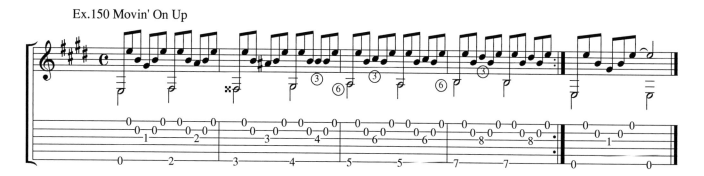

Arpeggios and String Crossing

String Crossing Introduction; Open String Exercises

String crossing occurs when the right-hand shifts (from the elbow) so that the fingers can play on a different string set and keep the same basic right-hand position.

Many arpeggio patterns require string crossing. Some guitarists prefer to use string crossing so the stronger fingers of the right hand (**i,m**) play an arpeggio pattern.

If you play **p,i,m** on the 6th, 5th and 4th strings and then play **p,i,m** on the 3rd, 2nd and 1st string, your right hand would use string crossing to move **i** from the 5th string to the 2nd string a distance of four strings. See Ex.151 below.

Always shift from the elbow (not the wrist) so that your basic right-hand position remains the same. Do the open string exercises below slowly. Be sensitive to the shift from the elbow.

Arpeggios and String Crossing

String Crossing; Exercises

Ex.155 Crossing the Great Divide - p i m

Arpeggio Sweeps

Introduction; Arpeggio Sweeps with **p**

An arpeggio sweep is the rapid playing of two or more strings in a single movement with a finger or the thumb.

The rapid sweeping of the thumb or fingers across the strings (arpeggiate) is notated by a wavy vertical line or sometimes a curved vertical line before a chord (see Ex. 156 below).

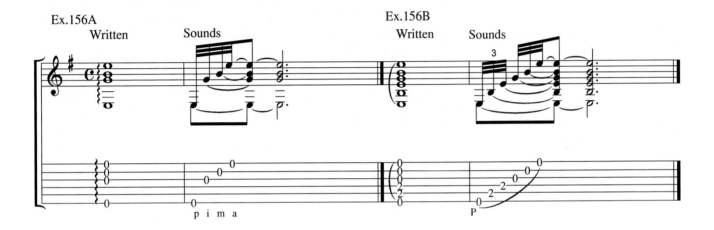

The chord is usually arpeggiated starting from the bass strings and going to the treble strings. If the chord to be arpeggiated has more than four notes a sweep must be used (usually with **p**).

There are many ways chords can be arpeggiated. Sometimes the back of the fingernails (finger sweeps) or thumbnail arpeggiate chords or one of the fingers sweeps up from the treble strings in a rapid rest stroke. In this section we will cover some of the common ways to arpeggiate chords.

Arpeggio Sweeps with **p**

Look at Ex. 156-B above. The Em chord can be arpeggiated (strummed so the individual notes of the chord can be heard) with **p** alone. This is called the **p strum**.

To play the **p strum**, make your right hand into a fist, resting the middle joint of the thumb against the middle joint of the index finger (see illustration 7 below).

Place the **p** tip against the 6th string and strum slowly across the open strings, briefly stopping on each string (**p** rest stroke) until you play all six strings. When you get to the treble strings dig in (apply more pressure to the strings) and rotate your wrist. Then speed up the arpeggio until there is no discernible pause between strings.

You can either use the flesh and nail of **p** or tilt the tip joint back and use flesh (the thumbtip) only.

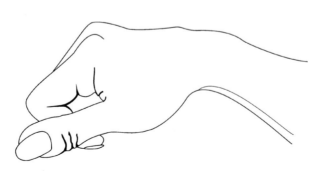

Arpeggio Sweeps

Arpeggio Sweeps with **p**; **p-strum** Exercises; the **p-sweep** Intro

P - Strum Ex.157

P - Strum Ex.158

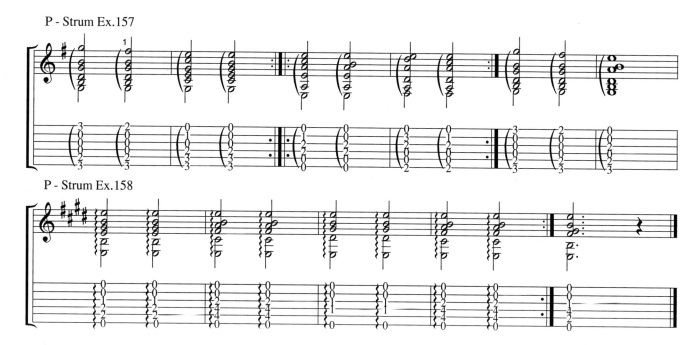

p-sweep and Fingers

One widely used technique to arpeggiate chords is the **p-sweep** on the bass strings while the fingers play the treble strings. The thumb (**p**) sweeps across two strings (usually the 5th and 4th) or three strings (the 6th, 5th and 4th).

To do the sweep the thumb must play rest stroke until it reached the string being played by **i** (usually the 3rd). Rest stroke with **p** requires a slight tilt of the hand and more flexion of the fingers.

To play the **p-sweep** and fingers first prepare your fingers on the treble strings as if you were playing **p.i.m.a** (**i** plays the 3rd, **m** the 2nd and **a** the 1st).

Try Ex. 159-A below. Keep your fingertips against the strings as you play the **p-sweep** on the 4th and 5th strings. Keep **p** relaxed; play **p** rest stoke on the 5th and **p** free stoke on the 4th. When **p** plays the 4th string and follows-through over the 3rd, play **i-m-a**. Ex. 159-B is the same on a different string set.

Now try Ex. 160 **p.p.p.i.m.a**. Here **p** plays rest stroke on the 6th and 5th and free stroke on the 4th. Again, hold the fingers securely against the treble strings until the **p-sweep** is completed.

In preliminary Ex. 159-162, the **p-sweep** is quick (not arpeggiated). Now in Ex. 163-166 separate (arpeggiate) the bass notes played by **p**. This can be done in Ex. 163 by making two movements with **p**; rest stroke on the 5th (slight pause) and then free stroke on the 4th.

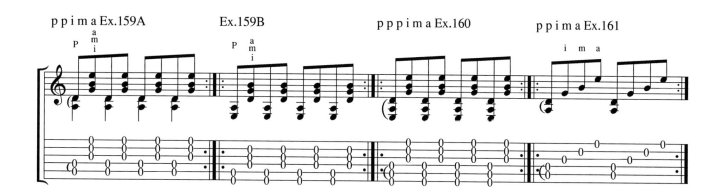

Arpeggio Sweeps

Arpeggio Sweeps with **p**; The **p-sweep** Exercises

In Ex. 162-166 below prepare **i,m,a** first before playing the **p-sweeps**. After practicing Ex. 166, do Ex. 157-158 again, this time with **p,p,p,i,m,a**.

Ex. 167-168 are short music pieces that use the **p-sweep** in an arpeggio pattern.

Arpeggio Sweeps

Arpeggio Sweeps with Fingers; The **m-sweep**, **a-sweep** Exercises

Arpeggio Sweeps with fingers are a rare but effective arpeggio technique. To play an arpeggio sweep with a finger simply prepare any finger on one of the treble strings and sweep upward across all the strings from the trebles to the basses.

The most common finger sweep is the **a-sweep**. Prepare the **a** fingertip against the 1st string. Without changing your basic wrist and hand position (move the arm from the elbow), strum **a** *rapidly up across all six strings*.

Below are some exercises and short music exercises for upward sweeps.

Other Arpeggios

Skipping Strings Between Adjacent Fingers

Some arpeggio patterns require skipping a string between adjacent fingers. Rarely, a skip of two strings may be required.

Sometimes you can use string crossing to compensate for an extended reach. This requires a fluid shift from the elbow back and forth throughout the arpeggio pattern. To minimize the distance of the string crossing shifts, position your hand so that the weaker finger (the **a** finger) has less reach.

Other Arpeggios

Consecutive Movement Principle

To play rapid arpeggios, you should use a different right-hand finger for each consecutive movement. By repeating any finger (two times in row) consecutively, you lose speed, create tension, and reduce follow-through and tone.

In the exercises below, you must use string crossing to avoid repeating a finger. This requires a fluid shift from the elbow back and forth throughout the arpeggio pattern.

Other Arpeggios

Five String Cross-over Arpeggio Form; **p.i.m.a.m.a.m.i**

You can use string crossing for a cross-over. This requires a fluid shift from the elbow back and forth throughout the arpeggio pattern when m crosses over to the 1st string and back.

To eliminate the string crossing shifts, position your hand so that the **a** finger is more flexed so **m** can reach the 1st string when crossing over.

Other Arpeggios
Using Arpeggio Patterns to Play Scales

Occasionally, right-hand arpeggio patterns are used to play scales. The scale notes are played on different strings so that the *right-hand pattern doesn't repeat on one string*. These are called **cross-string scale patterns**. Usually one of the notes in the scale is played open.

Ex. 188 below uses a diatonic scale pattern in the key of A major to play a short piece, "*Steppin' Up*".

The scales in Ex. 189-190 can be played very quickly.

Arpeggio Bass Patterns

Introduction; Travis Pick (Alternating Bass)

Playing arpeggios over a bass pattern is one of the important techniques a fingerstyle or classic guitarist can develop.

Two important bass accompaniment patterns that are similar but developed in different circumstances are the Travis Pick and the Alberti Bass.

The Travis Pick

The Travis Pick is named after country music star Merle Travis who grew up in Southwest Kentucky and was influenced by two great thumb-pickers; Ike Everly and Mose Rager. After Travis rose to fame in the 1940's, he (along with the great Chet Atkins) established the Travis Pick (or the Chet Atkins style) as one of the most important fingerstyle accompaniments in the guitar world.

The essence of the traditional thumb style is this - *the thumb alternates on the bass string playing a oom-pah (bass then strum) rhythm part while the fingers pick out chord notes (harmony part) and the melody.*

To get the percussive bass, the right hand dampens the bass strings near the bridge (palm mute or pizzicato) while the thumbpick pounds out a rhythm.

No one knows the exact origin of the Travis Pick but African-American blues and ragtime guitarists such as Leadbelly and Mississippi John Hurt are one influence. The early bluesmen played with their thumbs and a finger or two. This imitated the oom-pah style of the ragtime pianists left hand patterns.

The Travis Pick can be organized into two distinct bass patterns; the rotating bass and the *alternating bass.* Try the open-string exercises below.

Travis Pick - Rotating Bass   **Travis Pick-Alternating Bass**

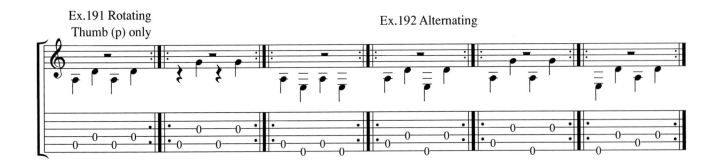

Arpeggio Bass Patterns

Travis Pick; Rotating Bass

The Travis Pick Rotating Bass is a bass pattern that alternates between only two chord notes. Usually the first bass note is the root of the chord and the second note is the fifth.

The Travis Pick exercises found here *may be played with any right-hand technique*; you don't have to use a thumbpick and mute the bass strings with the heel of your hand.

Later in Section two (on page 90) you will find a reference list with different arpeggios played with the Travis Pick.

Rotating Bass Arpeggio Exercises

75

Arpeggio Bass Patterns

Travis Pick; Alternating Bass

The Travis Pick alternating bass is a bass pattern that alternates between three different chord notes. Usually the first bass note is the root of the chord and the second note is the third or octave and the third note is the fifth.

Later in Section Two (on page 90) you will find a reference list with different arpeggios played with the Travis Pick.

Alternating Bass Arpeggio Exercises

Arpeggio Bass Patterns

Alberti Bass; Introduction and Exercises

Domenico Alberti (1710-1740) was a Venetian composer whose keyboard sonatas employed a bass pattern very similar to the Travis Pick. The left hand would play a three note alternating bass pattern (usually sixteenth notes) resembling a travis pick (alternating bass) played very quickly.

The Alberti Bass gained prominence as a keyboard technique and later was adopted by guitar composers such as Fernando Sor and Mauro Guiliani from the classic period.

To play a fast sixteenth note Alberti bass pattern the right-hand pattern could be; **p** on bass, **i** on 3rd string, **p** on alternate bass and **i** on 3rd string. By adding **i** to the alternating bass, a fast arpeggio accompaniment pattern can be created beneath the melody line.

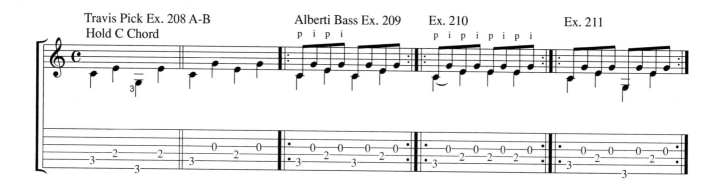

Giuliani's *120 Studies for Right-Hand Development*

Brief History & Outline; The Exercises - Introduction

One of the significant studies of right-hand arpeggios was written the virtuoso Viennese classic guitarist and composer Mauro Giuliani (1780-1829). As well as being a prolific guitar composer, his playing even impressed Beethoven.

Giuliani's *120 Studies for Right-Hand Development* feature many important arpeggio patterns that can easily be adapted to popular music today. 120 Studies includes chord exercises sections and bass parts with chords which will not be included in this arpeggio book.

The exercises are quite simple for the left hand. Hold C major chord for the first measure and a G7 chord for the second measure. The arpeggio patterns are repeated and end on the tonic (a C major chord).

The arpeggio forms have been edited so any single right hand finger doesn't repeat on consecutive notes. In many cases, this will require the ending C chord to be a single C bass note or a drawn out arpeggio of the final chord (see examples below). If you slow down the arpeggio pattern on the last repeat, the entire C major chord can also be played (as in the original).

Example - No.2 Original Ex.   Example - No.2 Edited Ex.

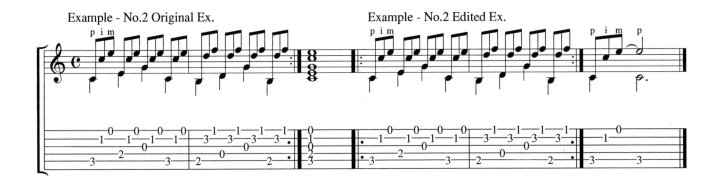

Example - No.5 Original Ex.5   Example - No.5 Edited Ex.

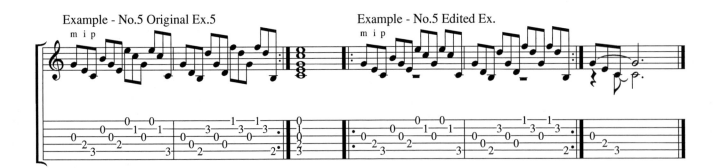

Giuliani's *120 Studies for Right-Hand Development*

The Excerpts

Giuliani's *120 Studies for Right-Hand Development*
The Excerpts

No. 25 through No. 89 are written in 2/4 time to save space. Each measure should be repeated and then the entire number repeated.

Giuliani's *120 Studies for Right-Hand Development*

The Excerpts

No. 36 through No. 50 are studies of the famous *Alberti Bass* pattern. A melody note or notes have been added above the pattern.

Giuliani's *120 Studies for Right–Hand Development*

The Excerpts

No. 36 through No. 50 are studies of the famous *Alberti Bass* pattern. A melody note or notes have been added above the pattern.

Giuliani's *120 Studies for Right-Hand Development*
The Excerpts

Giuliani's *120 Studies for Right–Hand Development*

The Excerpts

Giuliani's *120 Studies for Right-Hand Development*

The Excerpts

No. 98

No. 99

No. 100

No. 106

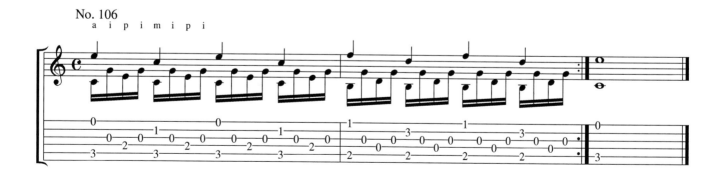

Commonly Used Arpeggios List

Forward Rolls; Backward Rolls

Here is a short list of commonly used arpeggio forms. The arpeggio forms are listed in the order they appear in this book. The forms are presented in a similar format as Giuliani's *120 Studies*. Use them as warm-up and review studies.

Commonly Used Arpeggios List

Backward Rolls; Tremolo; Alternation

Commonly Used Arpeggios List

Alternation; Arpeggios Without **p**; Forward-Backward Rolls

Commonly Used Arpeggios List

Forward-Backward Rolls; Backward-Forward Rolls; Cross-Over Rolls

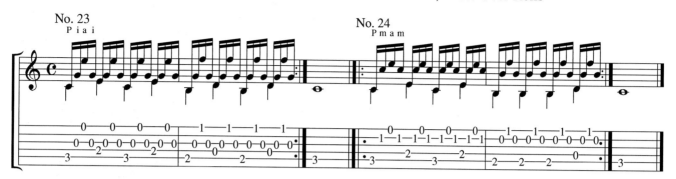

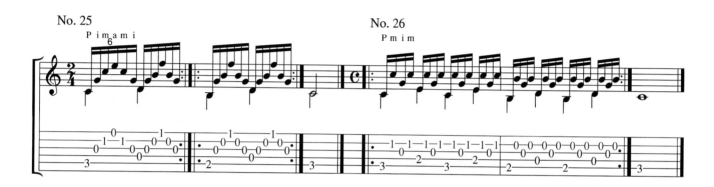

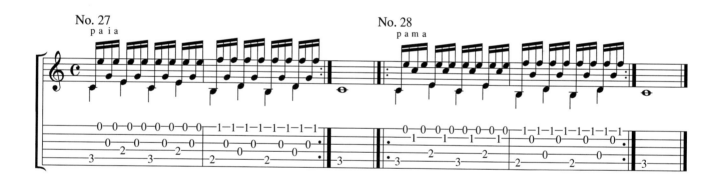

Travis Pick Arpeggio List
Comparing Rotating Bass & Alternating Bass

The next three pages have fifteen different Travis Pick patterns. The first pattern (labeled A) on the left is an arpeggio pattern using the rotating bass. The pattern on the same line on the right (labeled B) is exactly the same pattern using an alternating bass.

Travis Pick Arpeggio List
Comparing Rotating Bass & Alternating Bass

Travis Pick Arpeggio List
Comparing Rotating Bass & Alternating Bass

No Mo' Trouble Blues (Excerpt)

Travis Pick Song

From the album, True Blue
by R. Matteson

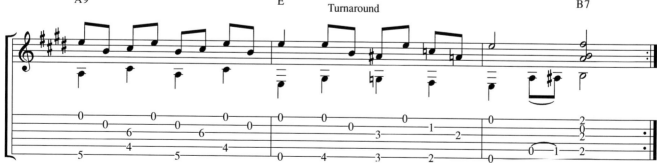

Freight Train

Travis Pick Song

Elizabeth Cotton
Arr. by R. Matteson

Intro: Slow Tempo   Accel. poco a poco (Speed up gradually)

Steady Tempo

BI - - - - - - -

BI - - - - - - - - -

County Blues in G

Travis Pick Song

by R. Matteson

County Blues in E

Travis Pick Song

by R. Matteson

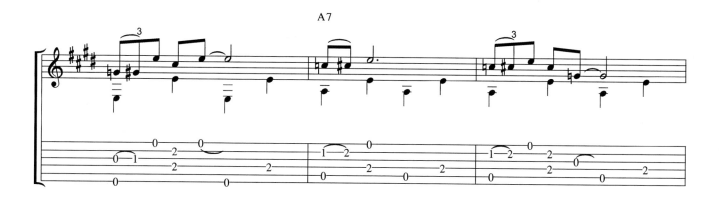

I Ain't Worried

Travis Pick Song

From the album "True Blue"
Composed by R. Matteson

A Ragtime March

Not Fast

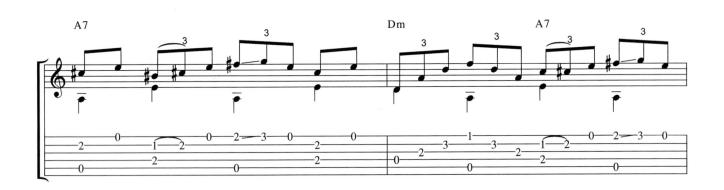

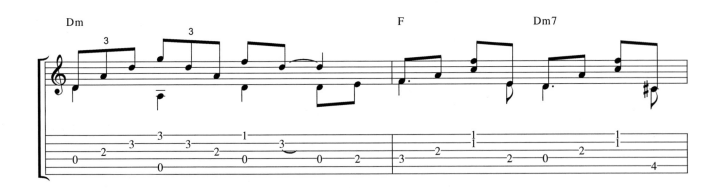

98

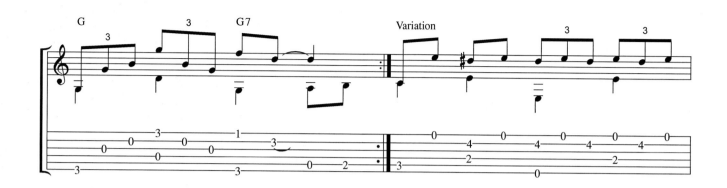

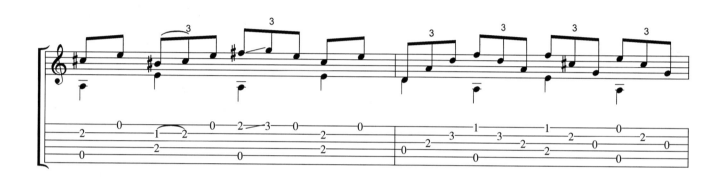

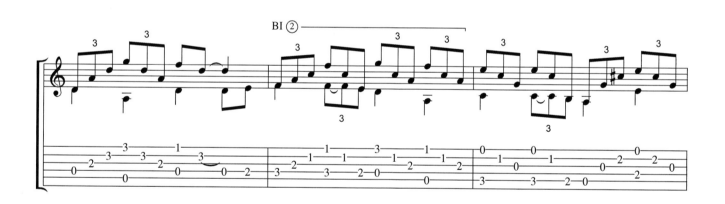

Arranging Popular Melodies Arpeggio Style

Most melodies can be arranged arpeggio style (with an arpeggio accompaniment). Simply take the melody and add an eighth note arpeggio pattern made up of chord notes below the melody line.

I have included two popular melodies; Amazing Grace and Greensleeves as examples of an arpeggio style arrangement.

Amazing Grace

Traditional American Hymn Tune; Arr. by R. Matteson

Arranging Popular Melodies Arpeggio Style

Greensleeves/What Child is This?

Arr. by R. Matteson

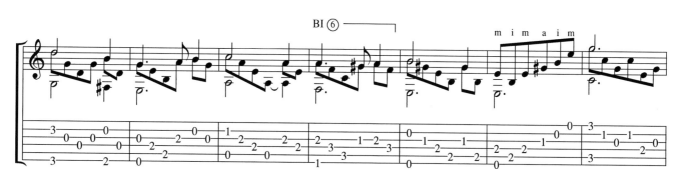

Lowdown Blues – TAB

a.i.m Study by Richard L. Matteson Jr. from "True Blue"

Lowdown Blues – TAB

a.i.m Study

DC al Coda

Lowdown Blues – TAB

From the Album "True Blue"

Composed by
Richard L. Matteson Jr.

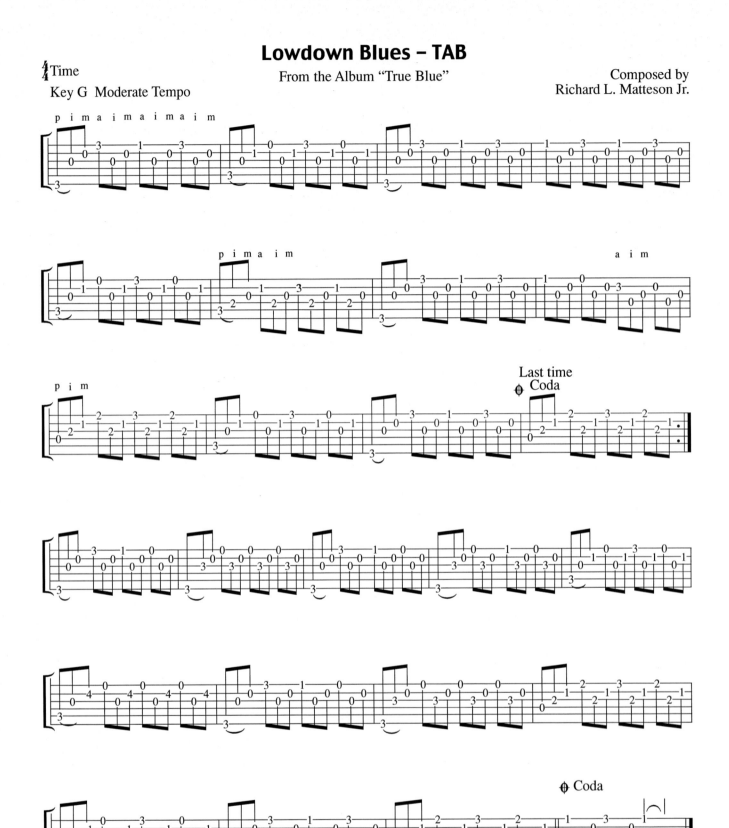

Iridescence

Composed by
Lawrence Long
Dedicated to Richard Matteson

Iridescence

Last Time
To Coda

Coda

Iridescence

Cantabile ♩= **72**

Key Em

by Lawrence Long

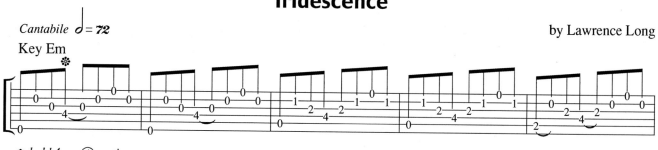

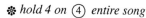

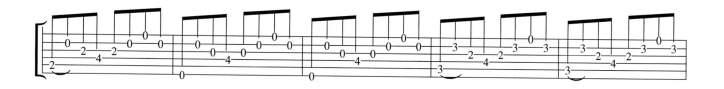

✤ *hold 4 on* ④ *entire song*

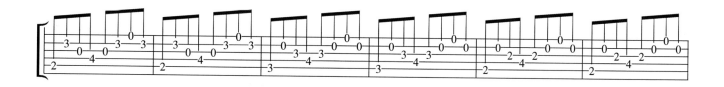

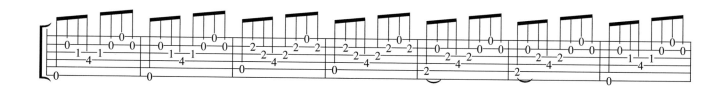

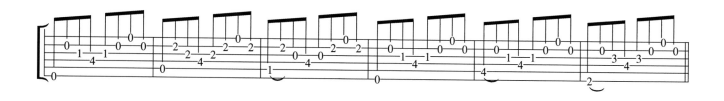

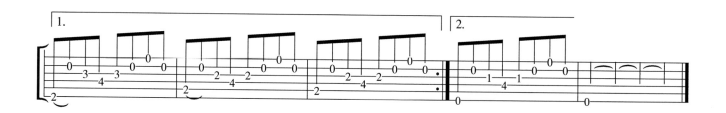

Popular Etude

by Lawrence Long

Popular Etude

Allegro

Key C

by Lawrence Long

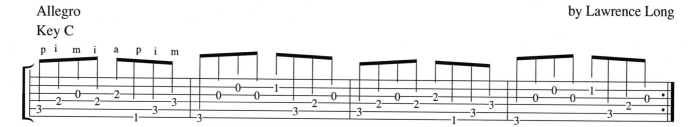

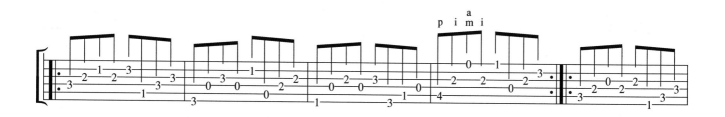

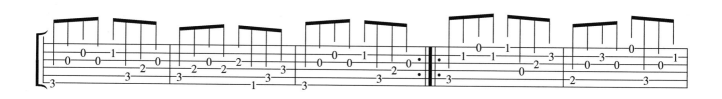

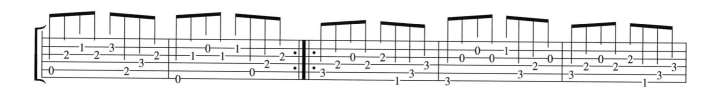

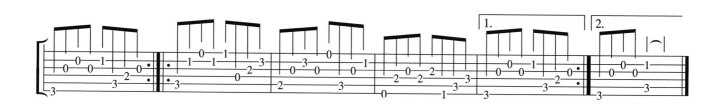

Recuerdos de la Alhambra

Tremolo Study (**p,a,m,i**)

F. Tarrega
Arr. and fingered
by R. Matteson

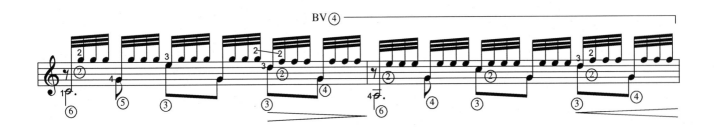

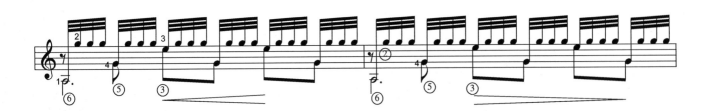

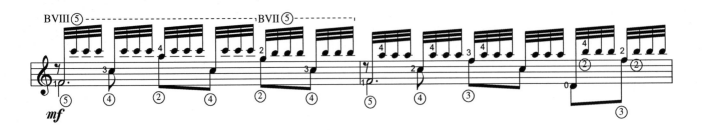

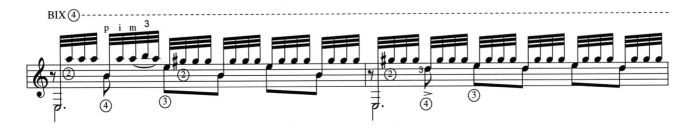

Recuerdos de la Alhambra

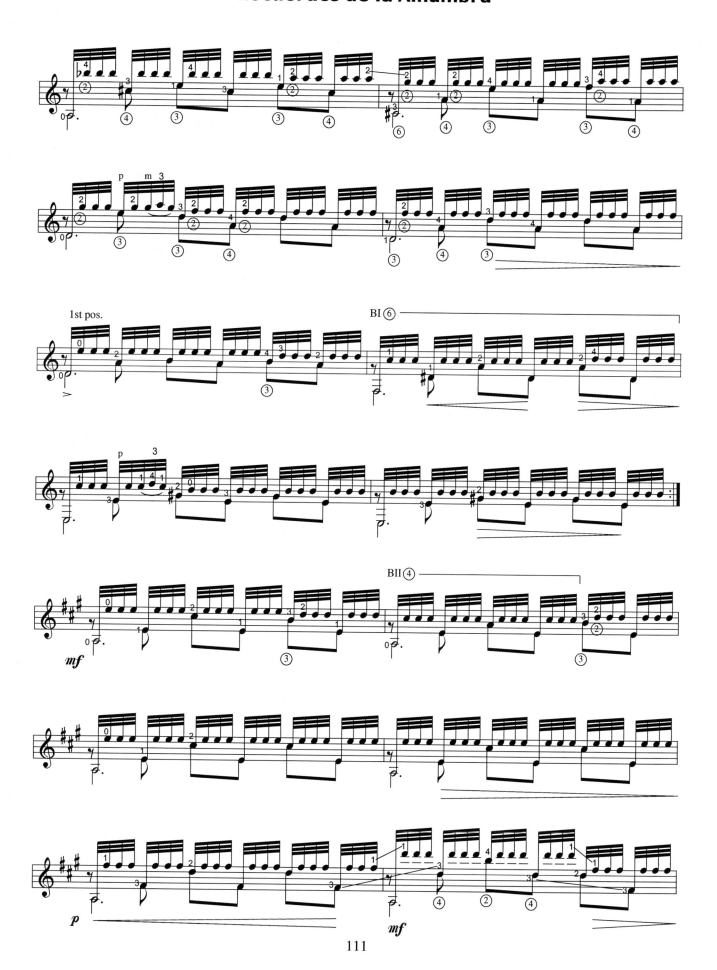

Recuerdos de la Alhambra

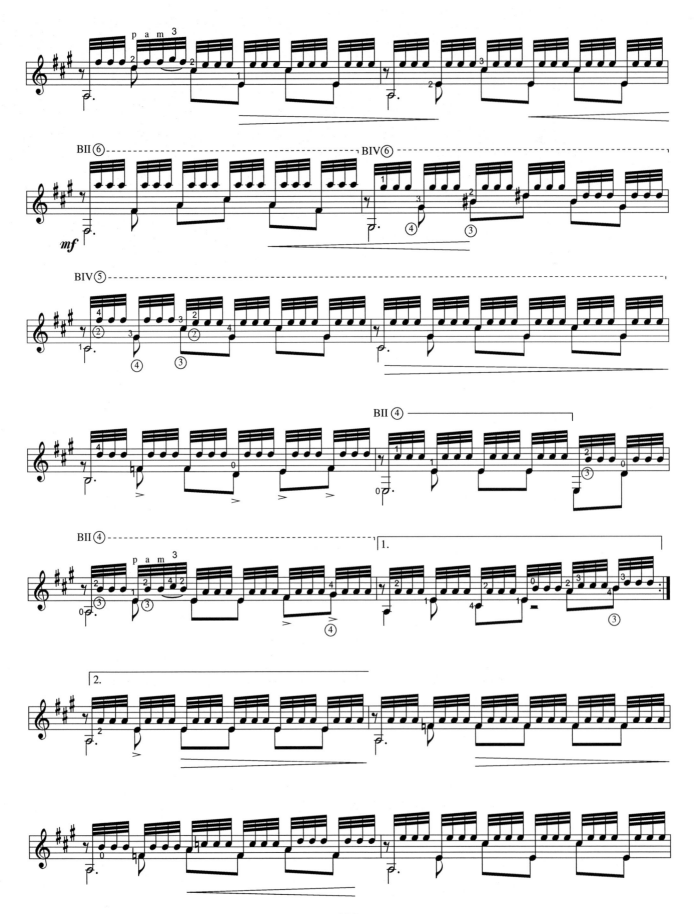

Recuerdos de la Alhambra

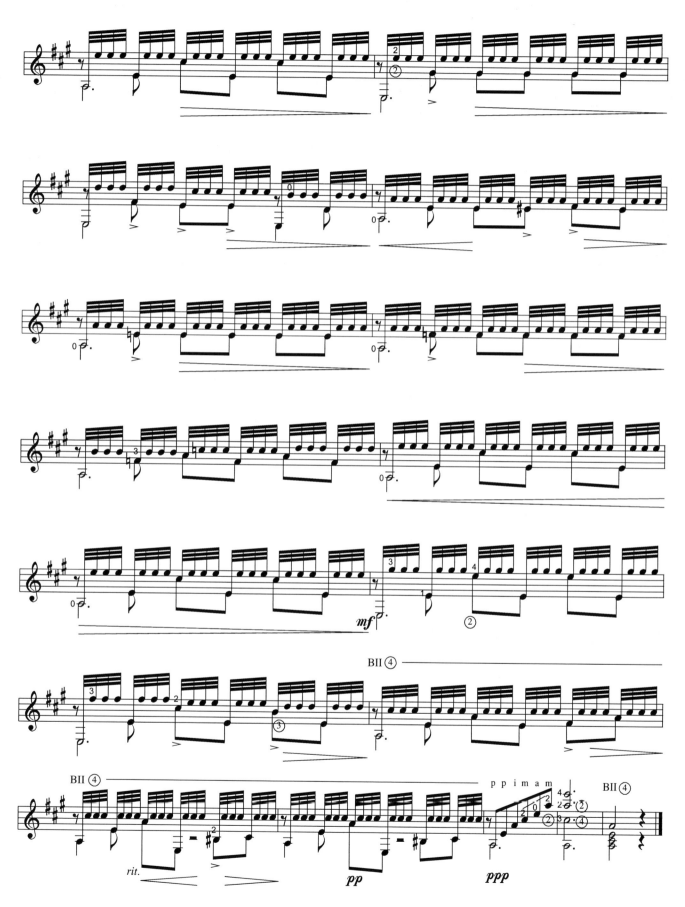

Recuerdos de la Alhambra

Tremolo Study (**p.a.m.i**)

F. Tarrega
Arr. and fingered
by R. Matteson

Key Am Andante

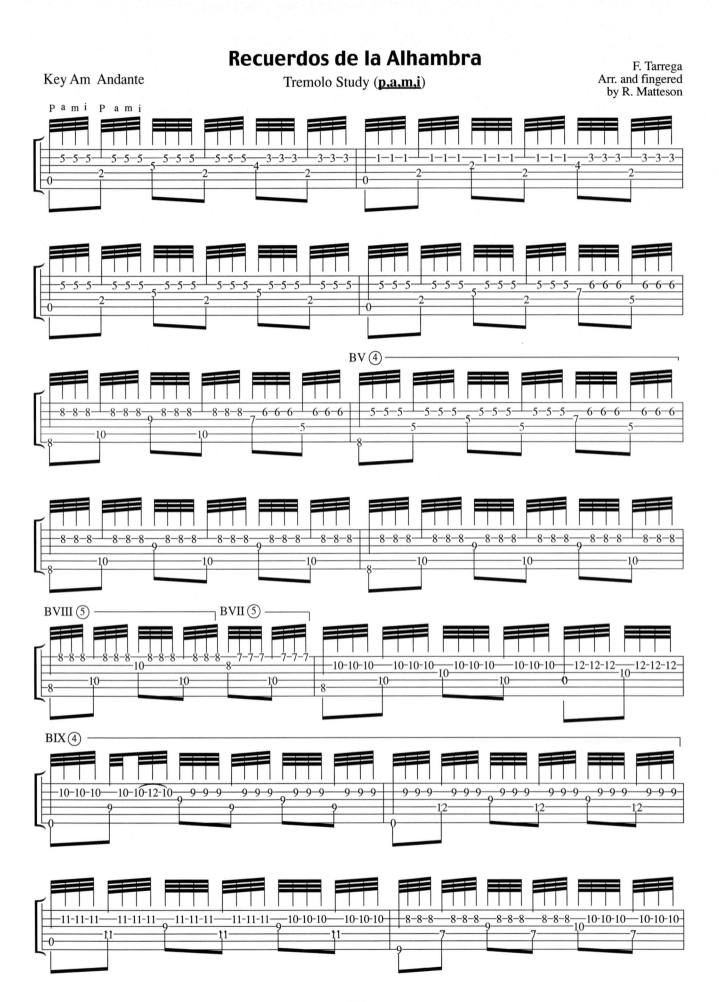

Recuerdos de la Alhambra

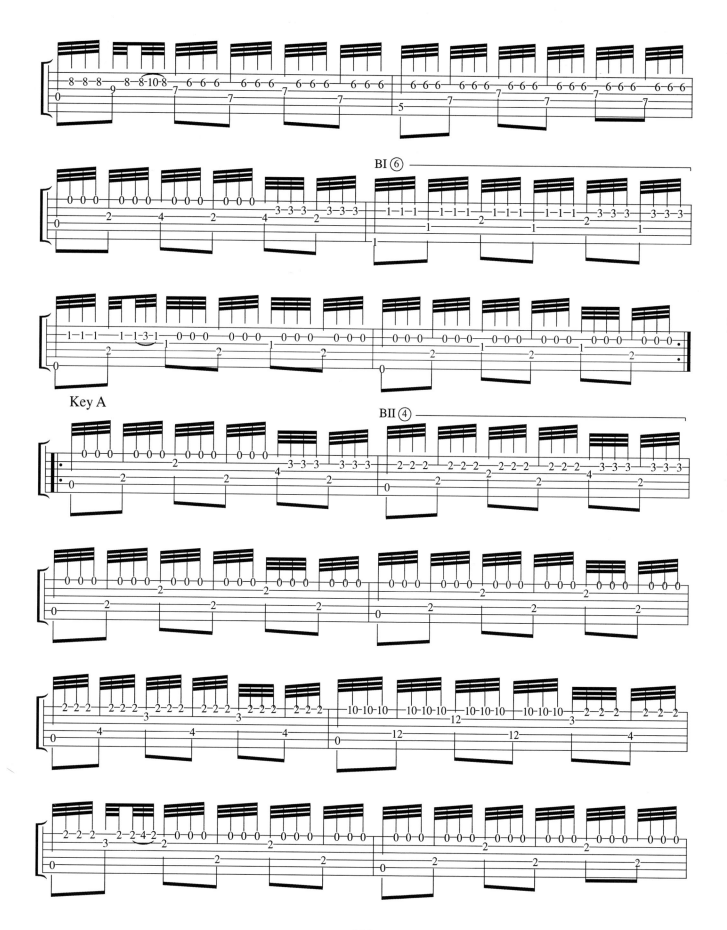

Recuerdos de la Alhambra

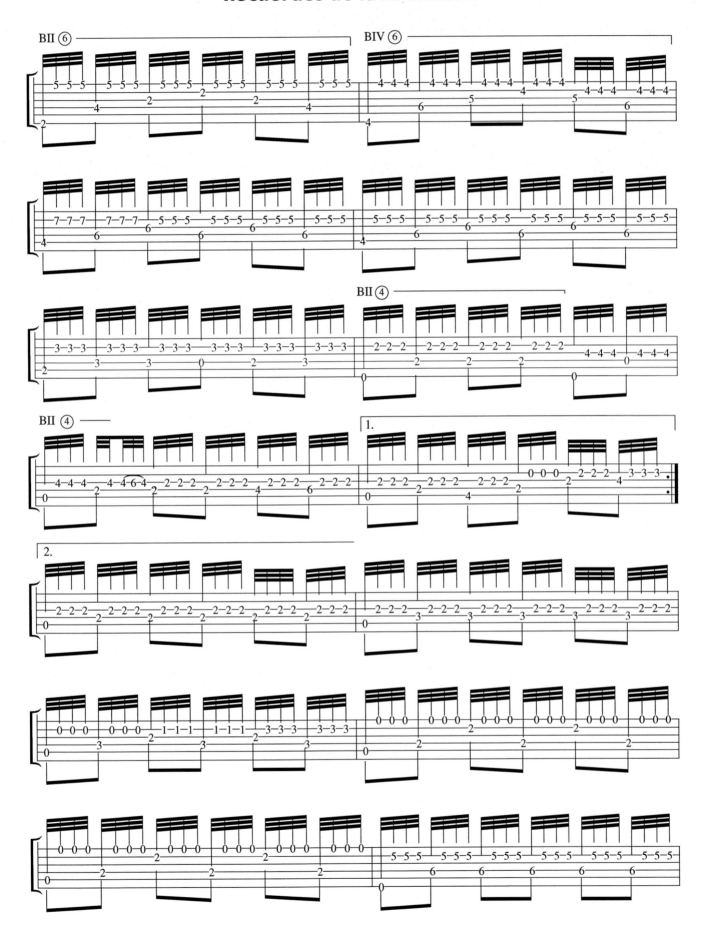

Recuerdos de la Alhambra

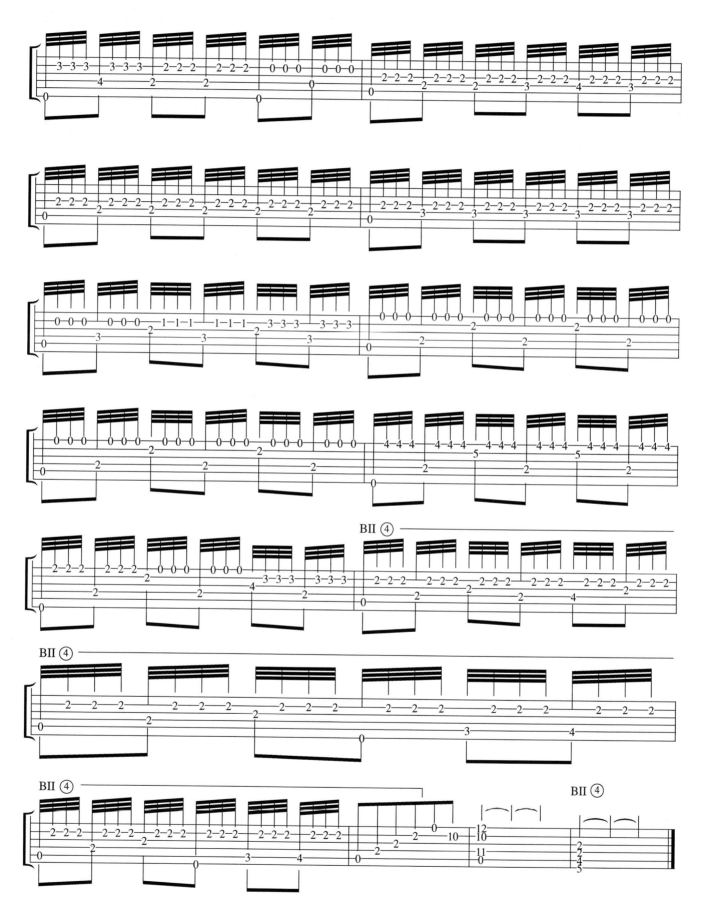

Study No. 17

a.m.i Study

F. Sor
Arr. and Fingered
by R. Matteson

Study No. 17

Study No. 17

Study No. 17

a.m.i Study

F. Sor
Arr. and Fingered
by R. Matteson

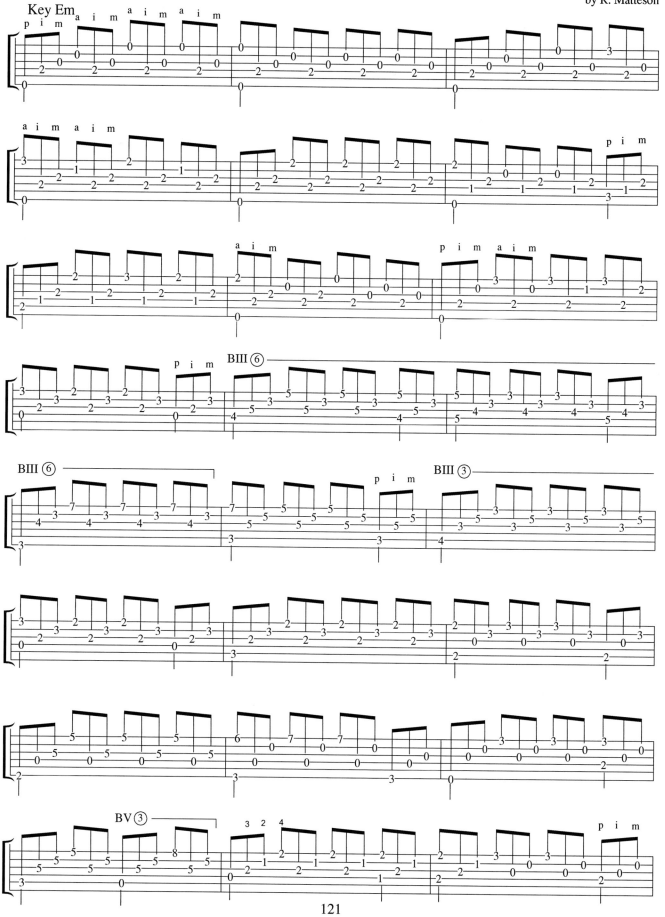

Study No. 17

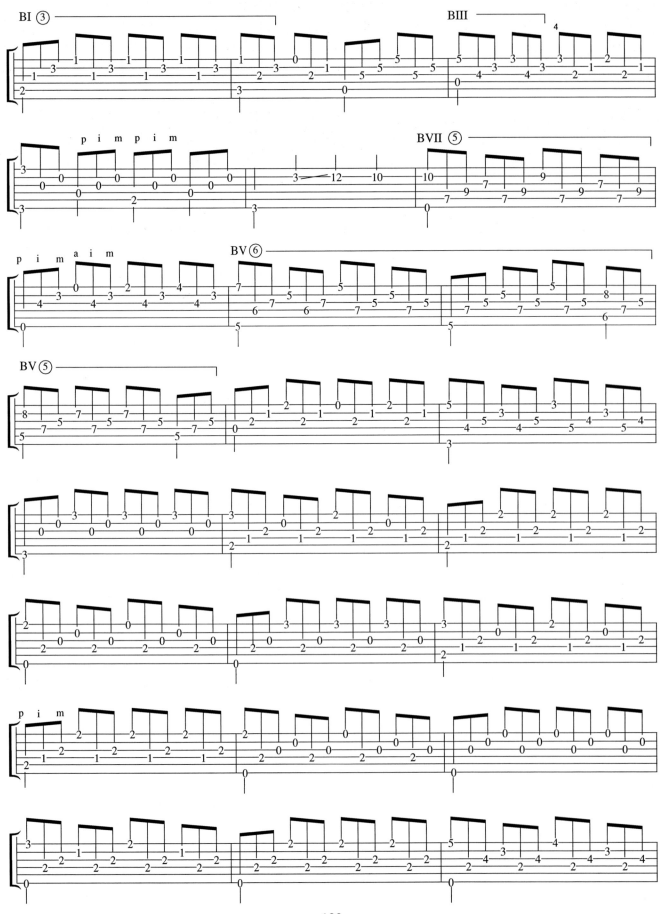

Study No. 17

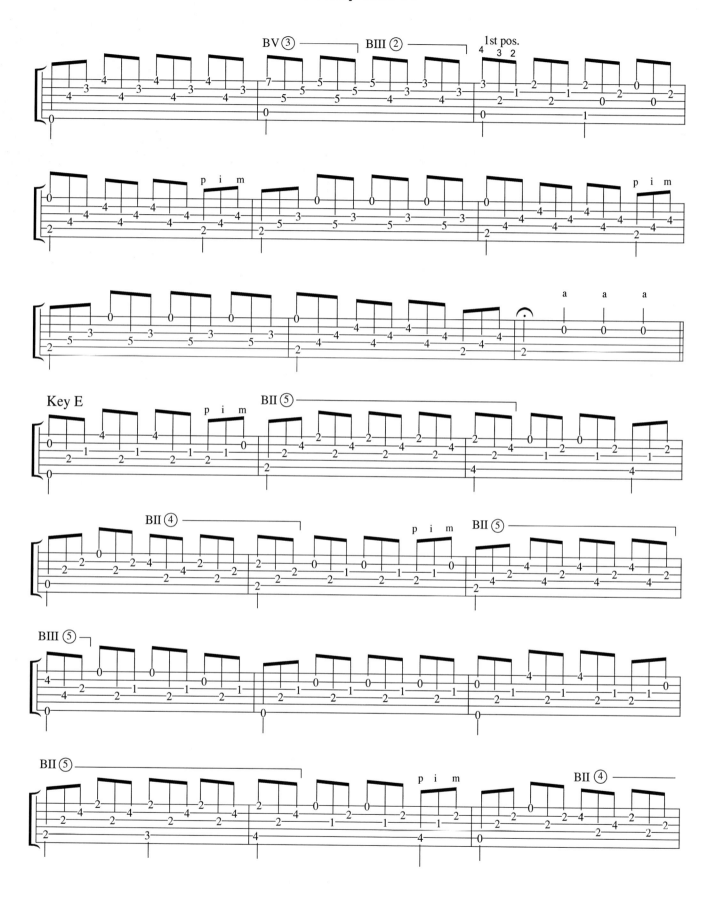

Study No. 17

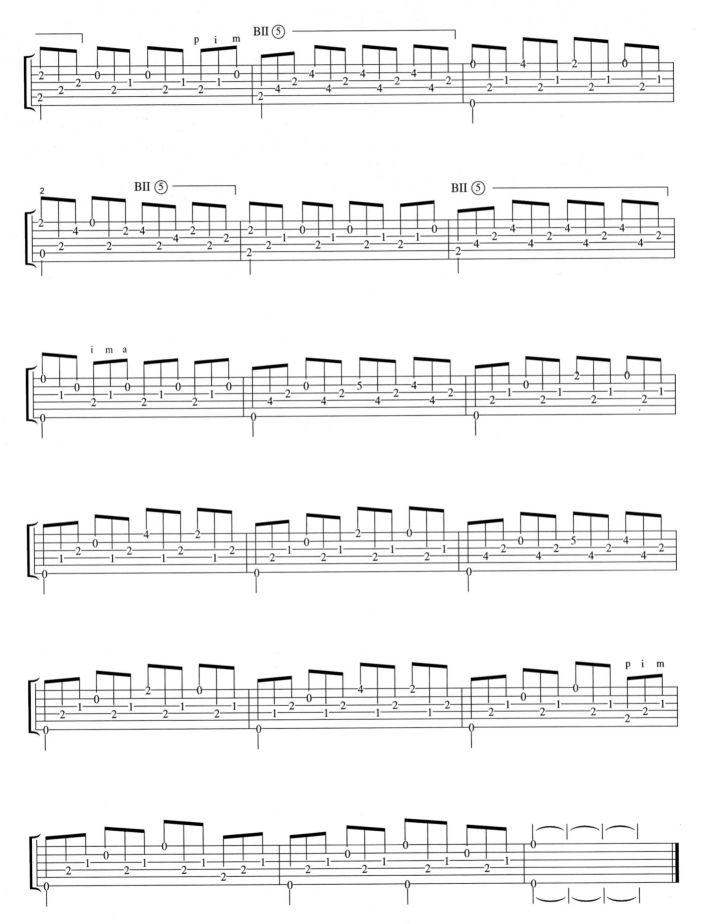

Study 7 – Allegro

M. Giuliani
Arr. R. Matteson Jr.

Study 7 – Allegro

M. Giuliani
Arr. R. Matteson Jr.

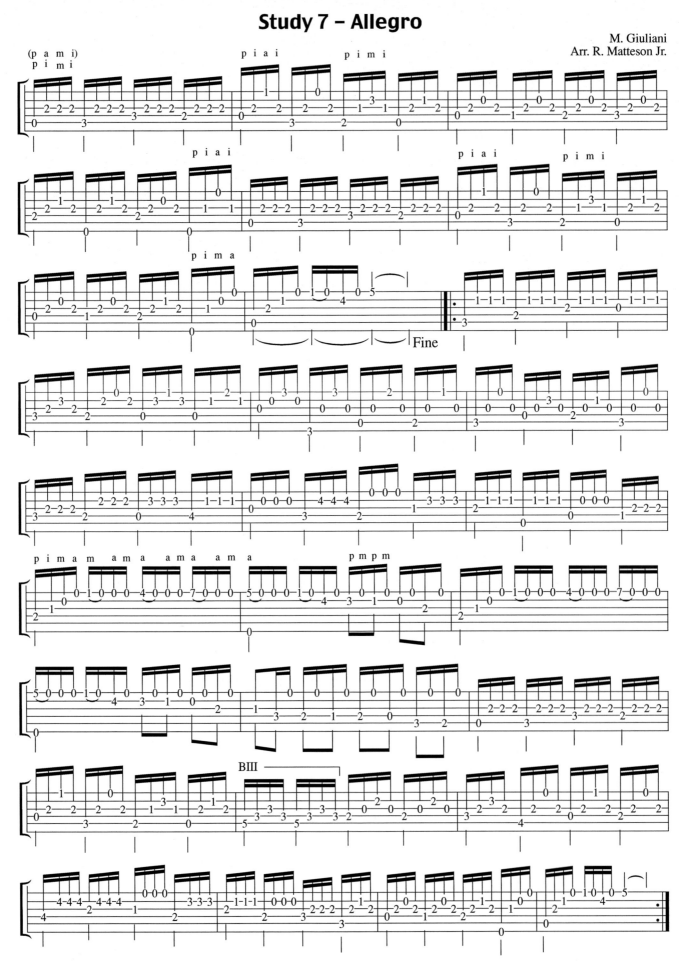

126

Spanish Ballad

a,m,i Study

Traditional
Arr. by R. Matteson

Spanish Ballad

Traditional
Arr. by R. Matteson

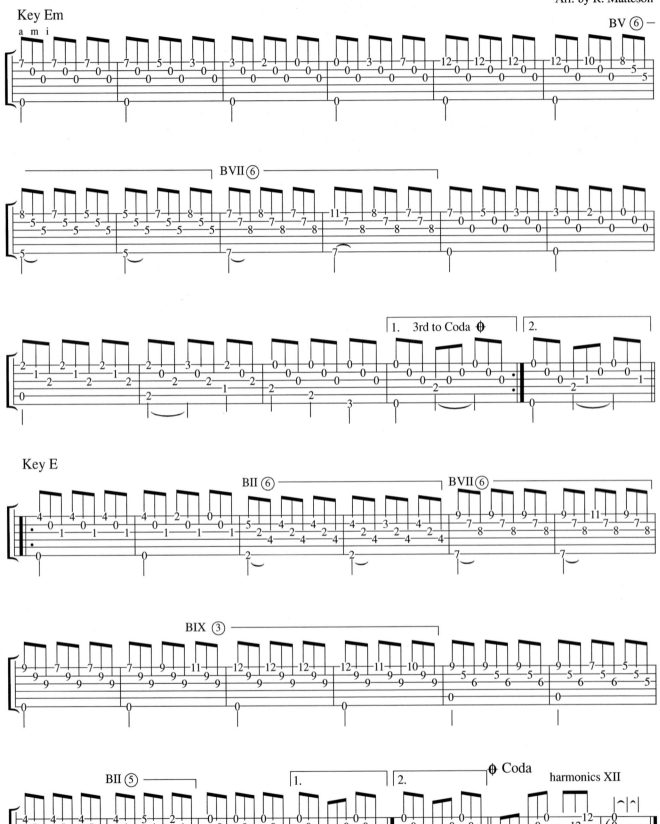

128

Prelude BWV 999

J. S. Bach
Arr. and Fingered
by R. Matteson

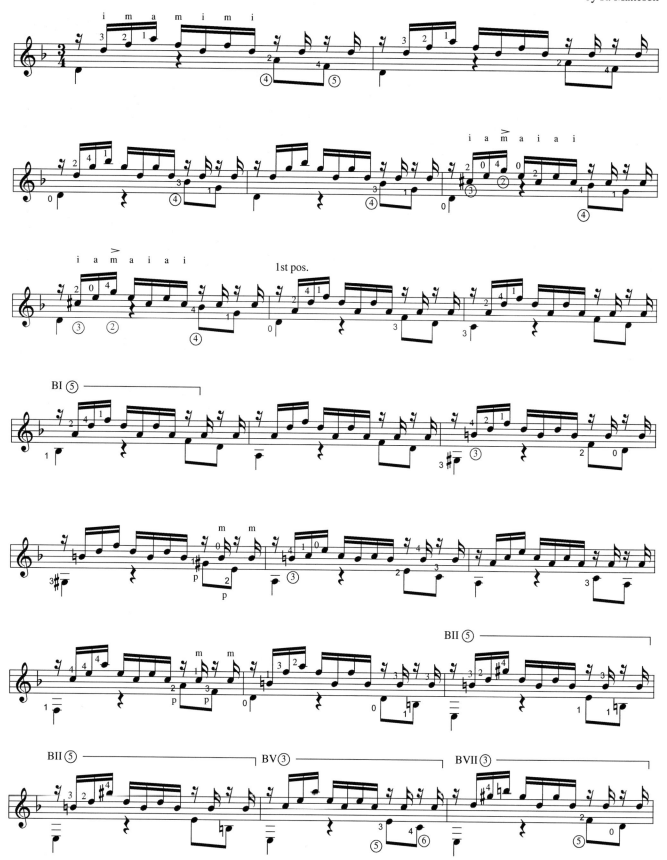

Prelude BWV 999

Prelude in Dm BWV 999

J. S. Bach
Arr. and Fingered
by R. Matteson

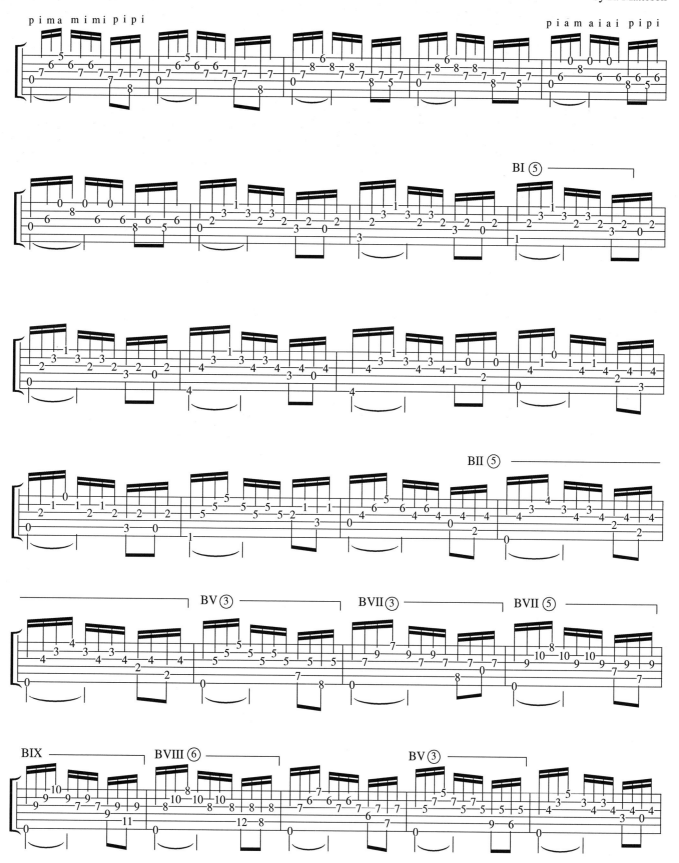

Prelude in Dm BWV 999

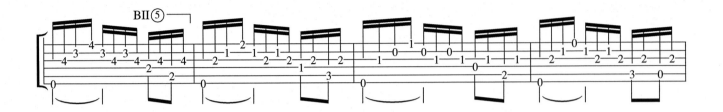

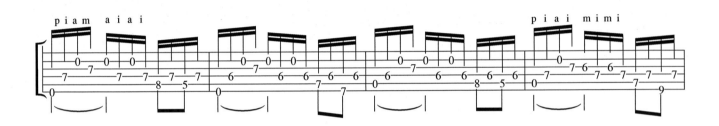

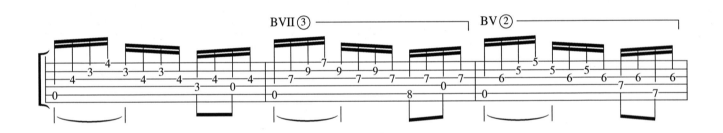

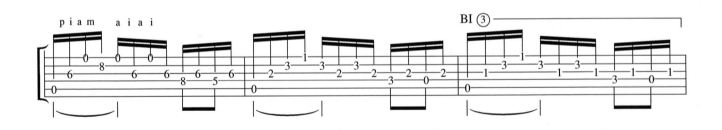

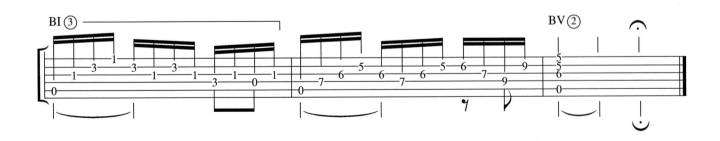

Leyenda – Preludio

I. Albeniz
Transcribed for guitar by
R. Matteson

Leyenda – Preludio

134

Leyenda – Preludio

Leyenda – Preludio

Leyenda – Preludio

I. Albeniz
Transcribed for guitar by
R. Matteson

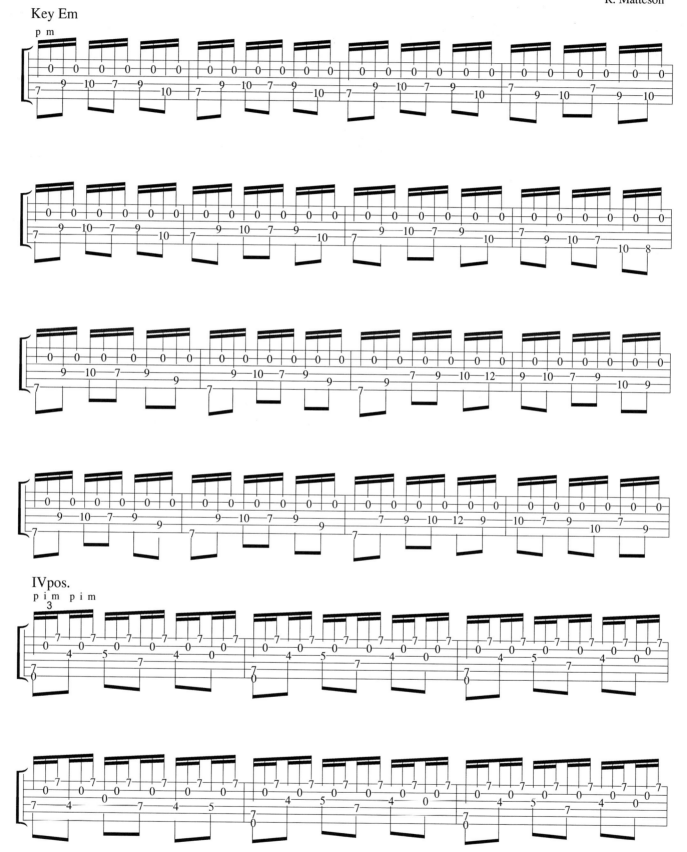

Leyenda – Preludio

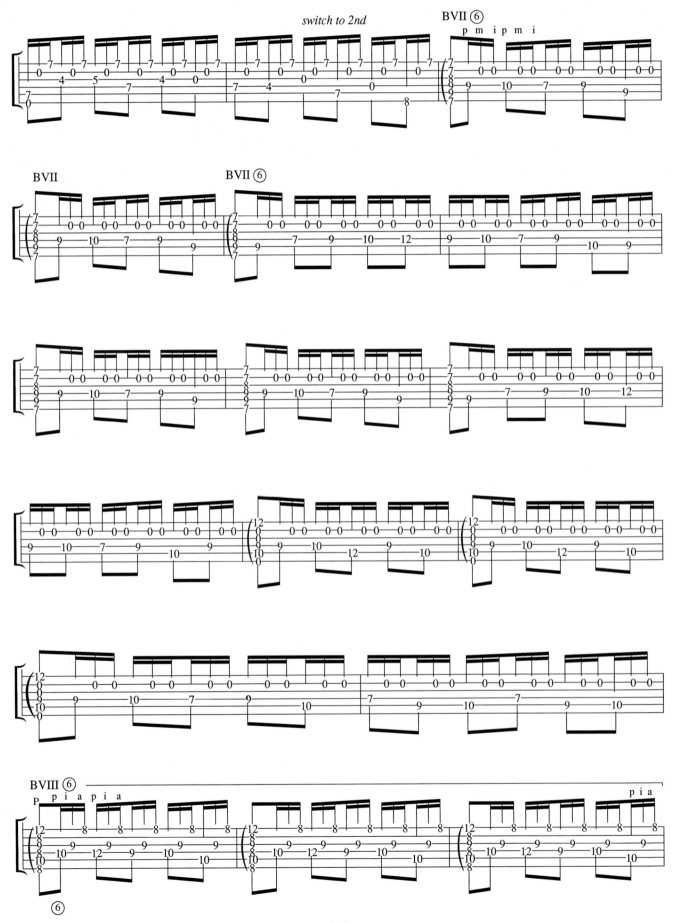

Leyenda – Preludio

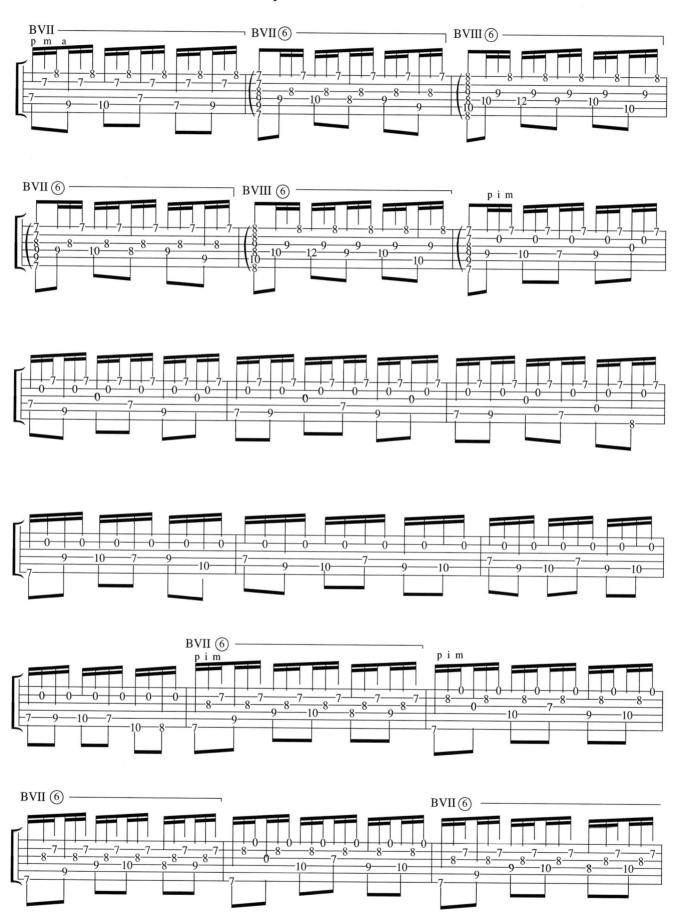

Leyenda – Preludio

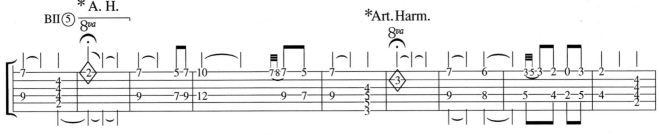

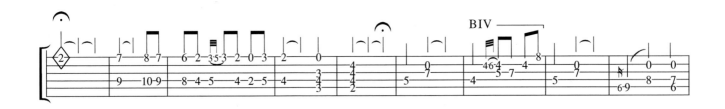

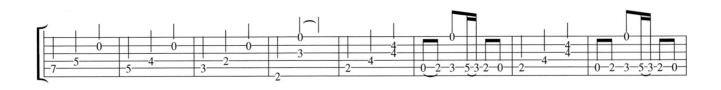

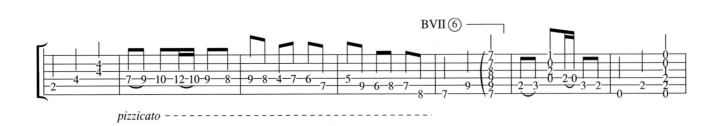

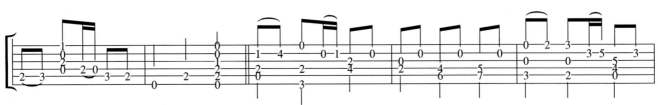

pizzicato -

* Play artificial harm with Rt hand 12 frets higher. Note Smalls 8va higher

Leyenda – Preludio

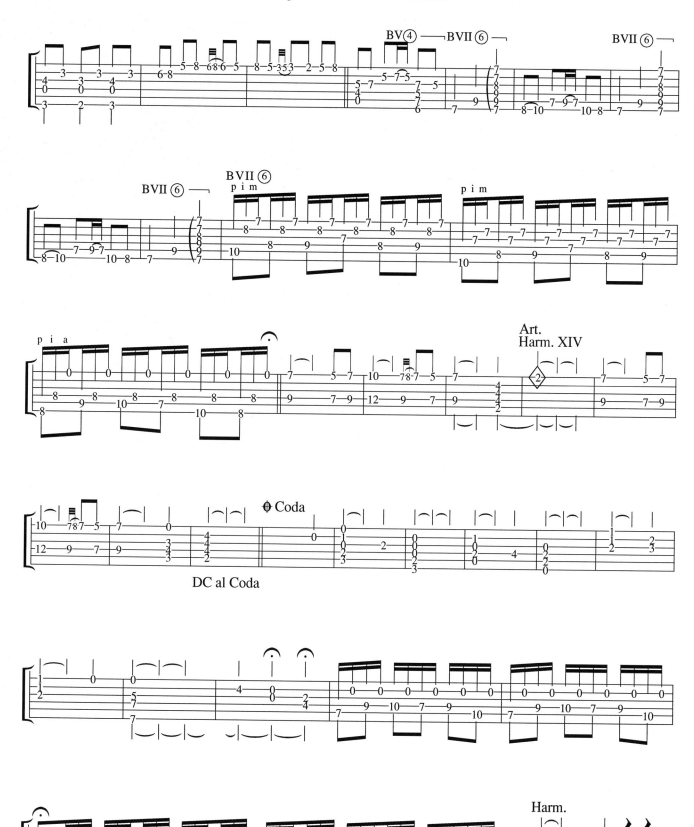

Allegro

p.i.m.a.m.i Study

Mauro Giuliani
(1780-1840)

142

Allegro

Mauro Giuliani
(1780-1840)

p,i,m,a,m,i Study

Key Em

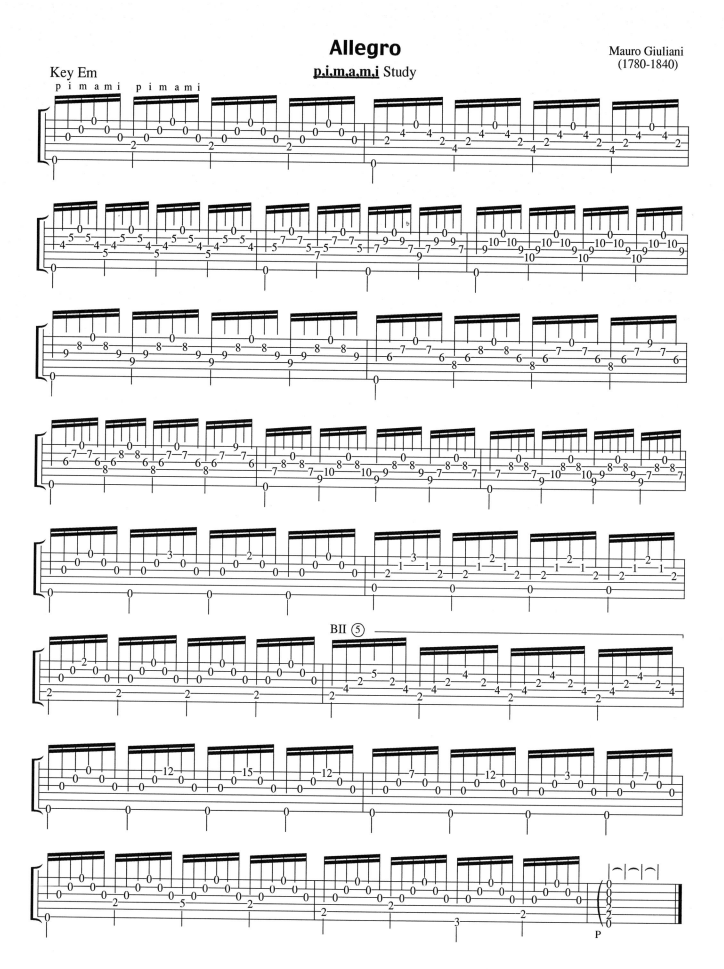

About the Author

Richard L. Matteson Jr. is president of the Piedmont Classic Guitar Society. A full-time guitar-teacher, writer, arranger and performer, he has dedicated his life to music education.

As a composer Matteson has written pieces commissioned by the Hendersonville Symphony, and has had his string guitar works performed in the PCGS Series at Salem College. He has performed his pieces and arrangements at the Dean Smith Center in Chapel Hill during half-time of a UNC basketball game, at the Merle Watson Memorial Festival in Wilkesboro, NC and at the Chet Atkins Appreciation Society in Nashville.

Matteson moved to Winston-Salem in 1986 to study and work with acclaimed classic guitar teacher Aaron Shearer. He is listed as a contribution editor in Shearer's *Learning the Classic Guitar*.

Most of the exercises in this book, were written by Matteson and tested by his students. The exercises reflect his interest in American music (folk songs, blues, pop and jazz), as well as flamenco and classical music.